Through
The Eyes
of
Dorothy

Through
The Eyes
of
Dorothy

Dorothy McIlvenna

authorHOUSE®

AuthorHouse™
1663 Liberty Drive
Bloomington, IN 47403
www.authorhouse.com
Phone: 1 (800) 839-8640

Published by AuthorHouse 04/28/2017

ISBN: 978-1-5246-8962-9 (sc)
ISBN: 978-1-5246-8963-6 (e)

Library of Congress Control Number: 2017906308

Print information available on the last page.

Any people depicted in stock imagery provided by Thinkstock are models,
and such images are being used for illustrative purposes only.
Certain stock imagery © Thinkstock.

This book is printed on acid-free paper.

Because of the dynamic nature of the Internet, any web addresses or links contained in
this book may have changed since publication and may no longer be valid. The views
expressed in this work are solely those of the author and do not necessarily reflect the
views of the publisher, and the publisher hereby disclaims any responsibility for them.

Contents

About The Author

Dorothy Shaul was born July 8, 1921 and died May 21, 2007. She married Robert McIlvenna October 20, 1941 her legacy:

<u>6 Children</u>: Dorothy, Robert, Kerry, Mary Ann, Phillip and Patrick.

<u>11 Grandchildren</u>: Jamie, Bambi, Jessie, Bridget, Brittany, Shawn, Jeffrey, Ashton, Christopher, Derek, and Kirsten.

<u>5 Great Grandchildren</u>: Robert (Bobby), Constance, Abigail, Chloe, and Tyler.

After raising her 6 kids she returned to school completing her G.E.D., then proceeded to college. On June 3, 1994, age 73, graduated with an 'Associate's Degree in Commercial Arts'. She worked several years helping produce an educational local Children's TV show called 'Daedal Doors' in Michigan. She had her own business of dog grooming in her home. She wrote 3 novels, many children's stories, drew her own illustrations, wrote music lyrics, one hymn and lots of poetry. She wrote two stories for young teenagers that she published herself.

Her legacy was for her books to be published for her family. After she passed it was decided to have her books published for the world to enjoy. This book is her book of Poetry, song lyrics, skits and essays. She also wrote children's stories, 3 Novels (Stamp of Approval, Peter's Plight, Time will Tell) and two teen books (The Secret Cave, The Runaway).

She was a very loving mother who said her Rosary daily helping her family thru many trials on her knees in prayer. She is now with the Lord but her legacy thru her books and family will live on forever.

A Blunder, By Thunder!!

The king sat beneath his golden crown,
He wore on his face a royal frown.
Worried about his terrible blunder,
His velvet cloak hid a problem down under.

He faced his court with a kingly blush,
The color as bright as a royal flush.
Would they discover his awful mistake?
The thought made his highness shiver and shake.

He dare not stand, for it would show!
He dare not let his subjects know!
His kingdom would proclaim the news;
When the king got dressed...
He forgets his shoes.

(c) 1987

A Christmas Wish

I wish that I could capture
      the glow from the Christmas star.
I'd catch it like a firefly
      and place it in a jar.

Then when your days are gloomy
      and life seems oh so dark,
I'd let you hold my magic jar
      to give your life a spark!

(c) 1995

A Giant Fell

A giant maple stood tall and staid
for forty years providing shade
with outstretched leafy arms;
   a nesting place for birds...
   a playground for squirrels...
A haven for them one and all.

Then came the day saws bit deep.
Limbs fell slowly in a heap.
     I heard it moan,
     life's sap seeping,
     I sat weeping,
That day I watched the giant fall.

What's this I see? I do declare!
Is that your offspring growing there?
       Life goes on!

(c) 1995

A Mother's Christmas Wish

In every mother's heart
    there is a special place
Where she stores away the memories
    of the glow on a small child's face.

Of that very special moment,
    of the awakening Christmas morn.
The glow and tinsel of a gift
    before the wrappings torn.

The stockings that were filled
    with surprises, big and small.
The expectations, wonderment
    of what may next befall.

And so it is when we fall in love,
    with a sparkle in our eyes.
Our hearts are filled, like the stockings.
    We just see the stars in the sky.

Then after a while, like the toys we receive,
    that begin to get worn, grow old,
The sparkle goes out of the romance
    Our hearts lose their warmth, grow cold.

We forget to look for the sunshine,
     and life becomes very dull.
The load becomes Oh, so heavy,
     and it takes you both to pull.

That's the time to stop and remember
     How it was when your love was new.
Forget all your heartaches and problems,
     and begin your lives anew.

This wish I now make for my children
     can be seen quite easily.
Just close your eyes and look with your hearts,
     and then you will clearly see.

I wish that I could capture
     the glow from the Christmas star!
I'd catch it like a firefly
     and place it in a jar!

Then, when your days are gloomy,
     and life seems Oh, so dark,
I'd let you hold my magic jar
     to give your lives a spark!!

(c) 1978

A Simpler Life

Life was so much simpler
        when we gave the horse some hay.
        We hitched it to a wagon
                and slowly rode away.

There were no crowded highways,
        no fumes from gasoline,
                no orange barrels warning
                        of construction unforeseen.

A neighbor was a neighbor
        and a friend, a friend indeed.
                A family was a family
                        and we recognized the need.

Then children were just children,
        living childhood as they should.
                We could leave our doors unlocked,
                        knew the bad guys from the good.

We cannot turn the clock back,
        just store memories away
                of days when life was simpler,
                        when we gave the horse some hay.

(c) 1992

Alone and Lost

She was three,
alone and lost,
among strangers.
She had clung to her mother,
begging her not to leave.
Now she was gone:
She was three,
alone and lost.

        She walked away,
        Having o choice
        But to leave the child,
        the child of her' heart, her womb.
        These people, she prayed,
        would care for her baby
        Sha walked away
        Lost and alone.

She stood there
Choking back the tears,
one small finger in her mouth,
trying to be brave,
eyes large and prickly,
she would not cry.
She was three,
alone and lost.

Down a dark and dingy hall
she returned to the room she called home.
She stood there, silent with remorse.
At last the dam burst forth
the tears flowed, sobs tearing from her
heart.
Clutching the little shaggy doll.
So loved by her child,
She slumped to the floor
So lost and alone.

no longer cried herself to sleep,
still waiting, longingly for her mother.
Occasional visits were all she received,
Occasional trips for a day.
Her new family was kind,
but something was missing.
At times she still felt
alone and lost.

She had a new life.
New job, new friends
Still she could not claim her child.
Perhaps her daughter was better off.
As a mother she was a failure
In the wee hours of the morning
Guilt was a demon she lived with.
She was constantly aware of being
Lost and alone.

She was seven.
Other girls had a mother
And a father.
Where was her father?
She had only vague memories of him.
Why must it be this way?
Why must she still feel
Alone and lost?

> She was determined:
> She would regain custody.
> Somehow, somehow:
> She was a stronger person now,
> Ready to cope with motherhood,
> Finally able to support them both.
> She must try.
> Too long she had been
> Lost and alone.

She was nine.
Oh, joy of joys
She was with her mom again,
New school, new friends.
But what was wrong?
Her mom was a stranger.
Would they ever to close?
Would she always feel
Alone and lost?

The battle was over.
Never would she have to
Leave her child again.
Somehow she must bridge this emotional gap.
Her daughter was no longer a baby.
They must learn to know each other.
Never, never again would she want to feel
Lost and alone!

The years have passed.
The bonds that were stretched
To almost the breaking point
Are once more taut and tight
Mother and daughter—friends,
Their hearts entwined with love,
Alone and lost.

(c) 1987

An Eerie Night

The night was dark and eerie,
  the shadows long and tall.
    The moon was cold with warning,
      and I heard a night-bird call.

Then I saw them through my window
  as they rustled through the leaves.
    What were these fearful creatures?
    I shivered in my sleeves.

When came the pounding on my door,
  my heart forgot to beat.
  As I reached to turn the knob,
    I heard piercing shouts of
      "TRICK OR TREAT!"

(c) 1994

Angel

I only knew my first born son
        while he was in my womb.
I felt his little heart beat
        As he reached and stretched for room.

I never held him to my breast,
        Or saw his baby smile;
For he was only with us
        For such a short, short while.

God must have made him special
        For He chose him for his own.
He lifted him to heaven
        To be near His hallowed throne.

Our first born son, a child of love,
        Is deep within my heart.
And though so soon he left me,
        We are never far apart.

I hope someday I'll join him,
        In this heaven he calls home,
And pray that I'll be worthy
        So he will not be alone.

(c) 1979

Anguish

Thoughts tumble through my mind.

Swirling

Impish

Racing

Pushing

Shoving

Vying for attention thoughts.

"Go away," I cry, "let me sleep!"

(c) 1994

Anticipation

The night was dark, no stars in sight,
blankets of clouds covering light,
lovers on swelling edge of night,
Anticipating.

Close together on the quiet hill,
the restless wind sending chills
lovers cloaked in the nodding night
Anticipating.

Waiting breathlessly as opalescent
moon appears, shimmering incandescent.
Heads close together they gaze at the sphere.
Hearts overflowing, the moment here!

Werewolf lovers raise hairy faces
to sing their lunar tune.
Still holding claw-like hands they
howl at the silvery moon.

OW o--o-o-o-o o o o o o !!!!!!!!!!!

(c) 1998

Around the Corner

You said, "Around the corner,"
but you didn't tell me where.
I searched about my neighborhood,
Dodging snowflakes in the air.

When I had almost given up,
A spot of yellow caught my eye.
As I picked the tiny Dandelion,
The sun burst from the sky.

It covered my Forsythia;
The grass was green and bright.
My world emerged with beauty;
My heart filled with delight.

I smelled the fragrant Lilacs,
Heard the songbirds sing.
At last I'd found the corner;
Discovered it was Spring!

(c) 1994

Attitudes

Life is what we make of it
    our attitude's the key;
        when viewing daily duties
        or opportunities

Greet each day with laughter
    or let the clouds seep through.
        Grasp each precious moment
        as a jewel or lose it, too.

Yes, life is what we make of it.
    It should be all worthwhile,
        just wipe away the teardrops,
        then practice how to smile.

(c) 1993

The American Plan
To stay fit and healthy
and make doctors wealthy.

(c) 1993

Auto-Respect

I am a car, they say I'm a Junker.
Sometimes called a blankety-blank clunker.
Do they care if I'm growing old?
That sometimes my engine is very cold?
When I am thirsty, do they give me oil,
or offer me water, unless I boil?

NO RESPECT!

There was a time when I was new,
painted a beautiful shade of blue;
My chrome was shiny, my windows clear,
My lights all worked, both front and rear,
My engine was clean, my oil didn't leak,
My tires were new, my brakes didn't squeak.
My muffler was quiet, my horn was loud.
My owner and I were both very proud.

MUCH RESPECT!

Well, guess what happened not long ago;
A man told me something I didn't know.
He said I'm a classic, fit to restore.
They don't make cars like me anymore.
He promised to make me good as new.
Will paint me a lovely shade of blue.
I feel so happy, I feel so good,
I know when I'm finished, it certainly should

RESTORE RESPECT!

(c) 1983

Beauty

The birds may sing

the sun may shine

to brighten the long day through.

But the sweetest song

the prettiest flower

can never be compared to you.

(c) 1991

Before and After

(A Villanelle)

Could it be that I was here before?
Perhaps another time, another place.
When I die will I return once more?

Does death but open up another door,
Crossing to another land or space?
Could it be that I was here before?

Perhaps I stood upon a Hind-torn shore,
A different person with a different face.
When I die will I return once more?

Will I remember what transpired afore,
Lives I may have lived so long ago?
Could it be that I was here before?

This topic wise men study and explore.
Yet life, before and aft, cannot be traced.
When I die will I return once more?

This mystery is one we can't ignore,
But should not ponder long, in any case.
Yet, could it be that I was here before?
And when I die will I return once more?

(c) 1985

Behold: Wyoming

The Mighty Sculptor looked upon the land.
He chose a spot in northwest U.S.A.
He studied it, then soon began to plan
Wyoming as the way it is today.

His hands began to mold the mountains tall.
His fingers formed the valleys and the streams.
He caused the flow of rivers o'er the falls;
The source that would give power to His scheme.

When the Master stopped to rest and ponder,
His elbow pressed an indentation wide.
It proved to be a place of worth and wonder;
The ridge above became the "The Great Divide."

Upon the ridge the waters separate.
The rivers flow to oceans far away.
Below this mountain range there lies "The Basin;"
A desert where no man nor beast should stray.

Northwest are geysers, wonders to behold;
"Old Faithful" spurts with regularity.
Tourists come from miles and miles around
To view this place of creativity.

Here and there throughout this wondrous state
You'll see the cattle graze contentedly.
Oil wells, spouting black gold, dot the prairie;
A truly fertile land, a horn of plenty!

Oh Wyoming, a place of wealth and beauty,
Your Rocky Mountains towering so tall,
Your national parks with thick green forests,
Your oil wells, mines; oh yes, you have it all!

(c) 1993

Betrayal

I trusted you

I thought you were my friend

Code of silence broken

Innermost secrets revealed

Words once spoken can never be recalled

Like raindrops in a puddle gossip spreads

I thought you were my friend

I trusted you

What's that you say?

You want forgiveness?

NO NEVER!

Not ever!

Never!

Wellll...

maybe someday

(c) 2002

Billy and Me

New acquaintances, still discovering each other's ways.
Each day brings new understanding, tolerance ...
Acquiring patience.
Though green, it's not from envy of my
freedom, the freedom he has never known.
Soon we will be friends, Billy and me.

(c) 1994

Blood-Letting

Sitting in the waiting room,
  waiting for my turn,
The thought of what I'm waiting for
  makes my stomach churn.

She will poke me with a needle,
  and I know it's necessary,
Yet it doesn't ease the tension.
  It's human nature to be wary.

At last my name is called
  and I struggle to my feet.
I walk into a little room
  ease myself into a seat.

Rolling up my sleeve she
  ties a band around my arm.
Telling me it shouldn't hurt,
  she smiles with all her charm.

In her hand she holds a needle;
  two feet long if it's an inch!
I do not watch, I close my eyes,
  then I feel a little pinch.

When I look upon the table
   I am shocked and I'm appalled!
So many vials of blood,
   OH, LORD!!! SHE TOOK IT ALL!!!

(c) 1985

Christmas 1942

My favorite tree, our wartime tree,
will linger long in memory.
It wasn't small, it wasn't grand,
tilting on its home made stand.

That string of lights with bulbs of white,
with red nail polish were painted bright.
Blue strips of cellophane shimmered in light.
On top a flag, with field of stars.
That patriotic tree of ours.

With cotton balls and candy canes
no other tree will be the same.
Yes this, our wartime Christmas tree
has lingered long in memory.

(c) 1997

Come Fly with Me

Come fly with me
    on wings of love.
        We'll tip-toe on
            the clouds above.

Take my hand
    we'll touch the sky
        No need to ask
            the how or why.

We'll pause to
    hear the angels sing
        drifting by on
            gossamer wings

Discover secrets
    still untold;
        words of wisdom
            will unfold.

I'll listen to them,
    share their mirth
        before we must
            return to earth.

Come fly with me.
Come fly with me.

(c) 1997

Contentment

The earth took a shower today,
washing the cobwebs away;
everything green
fresh bright and clean.
The earth took a shower today.

Our world is all smiley today.
The sun spread its warm golden glow.
I hear the birds sing
as they dry their wings,
Yes, the world is all smiley today.

Soon with the twilight's soft glow
the moon will be grinning I know,
as he sheds his light
on the nodding night,
giving comfort to earthlings below.

c) 1990

Could it Be

(Villanelle)

Could it be that I was here before?
Perhaps another time, another place.
When I die will I return once more?

Does death but open another door,
Crossing to another land or space?
Could it be that I was here before?

Perhaps I stood upon a wind-torn shore,
A different person with a different face.
When I die will I return once more?

Will I remember what transpired afore,
Lives I may have lived so long erased?
Could it be that I was here before?

This topic wise men study and explore,
Before and after life cannot be traced.
When I die will I return once more?

This mystery is one we can't ignore,
But should not ponder long, in any case.
Yet, could it be that I was here before,
And when I die will I return once more?

(c) 1985

Crossroads

Oh, would that as I walk life's rocky road,
Then I would bear with cheer, my heavy load.
That as I stumble on the roughened path,
My heart and soul may not be filled with wrath.
Then when I reach a crossroad, I may know
Which way to choose, which way that I must go.
Yet, how am I to know the right or wrong?
For winning may not let me hear the song!
Perhaps, perchance the loss may be the gain.
For do we not need sun as well as rain?
Does someone know, that I may understand?
If destiny, is it beforehand planned?

If this be true, the roads may cross once more,
To lead me to my destination's door.

(c) 1983 (c) 2001

Dawn to Dusk

I sit on my porch with my morning brew.
I breathe in the air so fresh and new.
The birds are singing, the sky hazy blue,
My day begins so right.

I sit in the shade of the old Oak tree,
With my feet propped up, a glass of ice tea.
A leisurely time for my dog and me.
The sun has reached its' height.

I sit on my porch in my rocking chair.
My thoughts drifting off with the evening air.
I soon forget all my troubles and care.
All on a in summers night

(c) 1987

Destiny

Our destiny that twists and turns
as God decrees, does not reveal
or hesitate, but winds and wanders
unknown trails to lead us to
a life ordained.

(c) 1995

Don't Weep

Don't weep for him
at journey's end.
He's free from pain
and peace descends.
       Don't weep for him.

Don't weep for us
we loved him so,
and yet we knew
that he must go.
       Don't weep for us.

Don't weep for me
for *I* am strong.
My path is chosen
life goes on.
       Don't weep for me.

(c) 1991

Enticement

What's that I hear?
     A night bird call.
It beckons, entices
     one and all.

What's that I see?
     A bright, new star.
It winks and blinks
     up there afar.

It seems to say
     "come join with me,
we'll have such fun
     just wait t and see."

I'll play among
     the stars and soar.
When morning closes
     nighttime's door
I'll slowly drift
     to earth once more.

(c) 2003

Equality

An eager bride
Her groom by her side,
Was willing to love to honor to cherish,
But not to obey, till they should perish,
So she turned and fled ⋯
In haste she sped...
With steps that were lighter,
To a future much brighter.
She possessed a need to always be free ...
Possessed a need for equality.

(c) 1995

Expectations

A babe is born, behold a brand new day.
A dream, a hope, a wonder to explore.
Forget the sleepless nights, they pass away.
This child projects a future and much more.
He represents a second chance to weigh.
To balance scales that may have tipped before.
Yet, let us not forget this child must be
True to himself, his dreams must be his own.
To make his own mistakes, he must be free.
To share, or if he chooses, be alone.
We must, however, guide and over-see,
Till time will lead him to his destiny.

Reward will come, but we must wait and plan.
Reward is when this child becomes a man.

(c) 1983

Family Tree

Our family tree would not be here,
    with its roots deep in the sod,
If the seeds, our love, had not been
    planted by the hand of GOD.

Its roots are our beginning
    reaching backward into time.
Its branches stretch toward heaven
    with our future family line.

Its trunk is our foundation,
    a tender heart within;
Love so strong that it must flow
    From limb, to limb, to limb.

Its heartbeat will be stronger
    with the passing of the years,
As it receives its nourishment
    from happiness and tears.

GOD blessed us with our children,
    seven branches on our tree.
Each one so important
    to their father and to me

Each contains a part of us,
          and those that passed before.
Each one has a little of
          What makes up family lore.

My tree no longer stands alone,
          with seedlings by its side,
It will soon become a forest
          And I speak of this with pride!

Now I close with pen in hand
          Words from such as me,
Any fool can write a rhyme,
          But HE alone can make a tree!!

(c) 1986

Fantasy

I fantasize of distant shores,
a land of beauty beckons me;
a place of glory, endless joy.
A Shangri-La where it may be.

I dream about your smiling face.
I run into your outstretched arms.
I feel secure in your embrace,
submitting to your magic charms.

And then I realize, my love
that I must face reality.
I'll keep this dream within my heart.
We'll meet again... in fantasy.

(c) 1993

Florida Beachcombers

I wander along a Florida beach.
What do I see?
People as far as the eye can reach,
gathering shells,
Beachcombers!

Gulls and Pelicans search sea and sand,
appetites keen.
Responding to every gesture of hand,
begging for food,
Beachcombers!

Waves roll in all frothy and white,
washing the shore.
Daybreak to sunset, all through the night
cleansing the sand.
Beachcombers!

Here am I 'neath a Florida sky
gathering shells,
feeding the birds, watching them fly,
I, too, have become a
Beachcomber!

(c) 1986

Foibles

Would you say you're always honest,
      or do you sometimes bend and sway?
Are you completely black and white,
      or do you live in shades of grey?

Do you always stop at stop signs,
      or do you sometimes coast on through?
And do you drive the posted speed
      just when a policeman's watching you?

When a clerk shorts you a dollar,
      would you make a fuss and shout it?
But if he hands you too much change, would you keep it,
      brag about it?

As you stand there by the river,
      a sign reminds you not to swim.
Yet you see someone is drowning,
      would you break the law for him?

I do not know what others do.
      I know I live in shades of grey.
Though it's wrong, I'm only human.
      Occasionally I bend and sway.

(c) 1984

Free?

Butterflies and elephants are free;
        to fly the sky
        to trod the earth,
to be as free as meant to be.
        Are they?

As eagles soar above the trees,
        monkeys climb,
        swing from vines,
whales and snails are free to swim the seas.
        Are they?

Politics decree that we are free
        to speak, to worship
        independently.
Yet, are we slaves to power, greed
        and money?
        Are we free,
        really free?
        Are we?

(c) 1994

Grand Children

They come in groups

or sometimes only one.
      They ask to play,
          want me to play,
              expecting me to join in fun.

"Come on play ball,

Oh, Grandma one more game."
      They do not know
          I cannot go
             the distance, I am not the same.

Yet, don't you see
the joy it brings to me,
      to send them home
         and be alone
           to keep them in my memory?

(c) 1992

Grumpy Old Man

I went down south to find the sun,
      to laugh and loaf, to have some fun.
But old man winter followed me.
      He chased the clouds to where I'd be.

He huffed and puffed with sheer delight,
      laughed and laughed with all his might.
His icy tears dripped from the trees,
      made it snow, if you please!

I shook my fist, said "let me be!"
      That grumpy old man wouldn't listen to me.
Instead he roared, louder than loud,
      blowing white powder all over the crowd.

Ignoring the beast I jumped into bed,
      pulled down the shades and covered my head.
Thought when his roar becomes a snore
      perhaps I'll see the sun once more.

(c) 1996

Guiding Light

Twinkle, twinkle, little star,
won't you guide me on my way,
through each night and every day,
though the journey may be far?

Point your finger to the place.
Take me where I long to be.
Mary's waiting there for me.
I long to see the Christ-child's face.

Twinkle, twinkle, star above,
I would kneel beside the cradle
enclosed there in the humble stable,
give to Him my gift of love.

Kneel upon the straw-strewn sod,
beside the royal robes of kings,
listen to the angels sing,
and touch the tiny hand of God.

(c) 1993

HE Listens

Sometimes when I am troubled
    I gaze at a starlit sky.
        The stars begin to sparkle
            like the twinkle in God's eye.

HE seems to say "I'm listening,
    I hear your every prayer.
        Don't worry, when you need me
            you know that I'll be there."

(c) 1991

He Took Me by the Hand (c) 1995

I stood in water to my knees,
my chariot flooded too,
in the fearful dark of night
desperate, wondering what to do.

Then he appeared before me
and took me by the hand
through streets and darkened passages
he led to higher dryer land.

A most unlikely savior;
an old bandana on his head,
his breath that smelled of liquor,
yet I followed as he led.

When as I tripped and stumbled
he caught me helped me stand,
always there to guide me
as he took me by my hand.

I felt a sense of sadness as
he spoke of losses he had known;
death had taken his one true love,
I sensed loneliness in his tone.

I asked, "How can I thank you?"
In softened tones I heard him say,
"Please pray for my dear mother,"
then he silently slipped away.

Hopes and Dreams

Old rocking chair, it beckons me, it calls.
It comforts me and soothes my weary bones.
Enfolded in its arms, I'm not alone,
my only friend within these lonely walls.
The sounds of stillness echo in the halls.
I rock and dream of lives I once have known,
mistakes I made for which I must atone.
Oh, gloom. Oh how these lonely days appall!

At last, I cry, "No more ... just let me be!
I'll shed the shroud that binds me to your arms!
I'm much too young, so much to do and see!
I'll not remain a captive to your charms!
I'll rise above ... release me set me free!
I vow I'll fill my days productively."

(c) 1999

How To Clear A Room

When the room is full of people
And there's clutter everywhere
And you want to make it tidy
And they just don't give a care,
If you follow my instructions
And be sure that you are heard,
It will clear the room quite quickly.
It consists of five short words.
Arise with notebook in your hand,
Saying "Let me read a Rhyme!"
It's amazing how they vanish!
It works most every time.

(c) 1984

Journeys

Where should we journey today?
Shall we travel on land or sea?
Should we climb the highest mountain
to look as far as we can see?

Should we go to the Painted Desert,
or view redwood trees so tall?
Let's seek out nature's beauty,
study creatures big and small.

Should we journey into Egypt?
Oh what stories we could tell.
We could trod the ancient ruins
and the pyramids as well.

We could go to darkest Africa,
watch the natives work and play.
Or how about Australia,
so very far away?

Perhaps we'll go to Germany,
to Italy or France,
where we could join in revelry,
eat and sing and dance.

*It matters not the journey
or the trips we never took,
for the fun is in the planning
from a geographic book!*

(c) 1991

Lancettes

I sit alone
at peace with myself.
Content
because I know,
within my heart that you are here
with me.

A boy with pole,
his line adrift, he waits.
Line tugs,
he reels, it's hooked.
He caught the one he lost before.
He grins.

Last Rose of Summer

Face of an angel, heart of a child,
Music filling her soul
Whirling, twirling leaping high
Stretching, perfecting Glissade and Jet'e
Toes lightly kissing the stage.
A talent to behold!

To bed at seven for much needed rest.
No time for play, no time for play.
Only the dance!

Hollywood beckoned, opportunity knocked.
"No! Too young!" her parents decreed.
Too late, too late, her childhood gone!
She floundered. What now?
No close friends. She didn't fit in.
Through shattered dreams the music lingered on.

Beauty faded as time drifted by.
Like the last rose of summer she withered and died.

(c) 2000

Let the Chains of Friendship Bind

If we would choose a different pace,
    erase the lines of bigotry,
    welcome unbiased symmetry,
there could be peace from race to race.

If God would strike us "color-blind"
    so we could view in just one hue,
    forget the skin-tones, blend shades anew,
    and let the chains of friendship bind,
would man speak freely from his heart,
    accept his neighbors points of view,
    walk a mile within his shoes,
support each other--not pull apart?

We cannot change what was before,
    cannot erase man's past mistakes,
    but we can use whatever it takes,
    bring harmony from shore to shore,
    with open mind be color-blind
and let the chains of friendship hind.

(c) 1992

Let There Be Peace

If I could wish for anything
and hope that it would culminate,
I'd wish the bells of peace would ring--
sounds of love would emanate.
        I'd wish for peace
        in the Middle East.

If I could cause the war to cease,
still the guns ... remove the hate...
fill all hearts with hope and peace,
sounds of cheer would escalate.
        I pray for peace
        in the Middle East.

May leaders of the hostile nations
realize this war is futile...
withdraw their weapons ... abandon stations...
stop the shed of blood so brutal ...
        Strive for peace
        in the Middle East.

May sons and daughters return to home,
joining hands with one another.
Let colors fly and free men roam,
Let it be known that we are brothers.
        Let there be peace
        in the Middle East.

(c) 1991

Lifeline

The ringing of the telephone,
disturbing me from solitude
forces me to rise from prone.
The welcome voice does not intrude.

An offering of hope and prayer,
wishing me a swift recovery,
informing me of current affairs,
awakening me to new discovery.
      A Lifeline.
I know how truly I am blessed
because of God and prayer,
because of family and friends,
encouragement from those that care.

Now I will pass the lifeline, too;
with a smile ... reaching for the phone,
a greeting card ... a prayer will do,
to help someone to rise from prone.
      A Lifeline.

(c) 1993

Limericks

There was a young man from Duluth
couldn't tell a lie from the truth.
His stories at best,
were nothing but jest,
And often were grossly uncouth.

Larry and Gerry and Terry
All had their caps set for Mary.
For Mary, you see
was easy and free
Dating each Tom, Dick and Harry.

Lost in Memory

He said to her, "Where are you?"
She answered, "I am here."
He shouted, "Please don't whisper,
you know I cannot hear."

In her loudest voice she answered,
as she hurried to his side.
It must be quite important,
her concern she couldn't hide.

When she reached him he was standing
by the window looking out.
She asked, "What is the matter?"
He replied, "No need to shout."

He continued, "I was thinking
of a night so long ago.
Remember that December
we were stranded in the snow?"

"Your old LaSalle quit running,"
reflectively she said.
"That was the night we pledged our love
and promised we would wed."

He placed his bony arm
across her shoulder tenderly.
They stood there close together
lost in memory.

(c) 1988

Lost Love

You touched me,
gently with your fingertips,
you stroked my troubled brow.
You kissed my eager lips.

You touched me
with the words I longed to hear.
You spoke to me of love
and hope ... dispelling all my fears.

You touched me
as you crept into my heart
when I most needed you,
promising that we would never part.

You touched me
as we strolled along the shore,
beneath a starlit sky,
pledging our true love forever more.

You touched me
as we strolled along the shore,
beneath a starlit sky,
pledging our true love forever more.

You left, for you were just not meant for me.
Tender moments, brief though they would be,
are locked within my heart because you see,
you touched me.

(c) 1997

Love

For every man there's a woman,
      for every woman a man.
No one is ever and island.
        It isn't part of God's plan.

For some love comes but briefly,
      like two birds passing in flight.
For others it lasts a life-time,
      filling each day and each night.

A love ever true, will endure and sustain
      the bittersweet moments of joy and pain.
A joining of spirits, a linking of hearts
      will lock them together, never to part.

(c) 1997

Mama was an Artist

Mama was an artist.
Mama went to school.
Mama did her lessons,
Followed every rule.

Mama learned techniques,
Developing a style.
Mama worked with charcoal,
sketching all the while.

Mama worked with colors,
Painting everything in sight.
hoarding nature's beauty
From morning into night.

The room was filled with pictures;
Still-life and landscapes, too.
Happilly with sketch pad
She drew and drew and drew.

Then came the final lesson
The teacher had assigned.
They must sketch a NAKED model,
and Mama didn't mind.

However, Mama's children
Passed opinions, one by one.
The first one only chuckled,
Said "It sounds like fun."

Two said "Goodness gracious,
Just take a lesser grade.
"Three thought it was funny,
Laughed at Mama's escapade.

Four was shocked and horrified
To consider such a plight.
Five had mixed emotions,
Wasn't sure if it was right.

The sixth one said "You live but once,
Give it all you've got.°
Papa didn't mind and said,
"Don't listen to that lot."

So off to school went Mama,
What to do she didn't know.
Then the problem solved itself
For the model didn't show!!

(c) 1986

McIlvenna's Menagerie

Someone once asked me why do we need pets?
They track up our floors and cause a commotion
Do they serve a purpose? I answered 'YOU BET!
They brighten our lives and stir up emotions.

When a little girls' lonely she'll find a friend
in a kitten to cuddle caress.
Someone to talk to about how she feels,
Put those feelings in words to expresses.

A cat is a prowler by nature
alert both night and day.
Farmers depend on their feline friends
To frighten those rodents away.

For a boy in the woods, a dog by his side
He will know he is never alone
His canine pet will protect him from harm
And will help him to find his way home.

For a lonely old man his dog is a friend
To take for a walk and feed
That aged old man wouldn't take that walk
If it wasn't for 'Fido' to lead.

For the blind he's not just a leader
He's his eyes and his guardian too.
He will lead his master to safety
Through places both familiar and new.

For the little lady who is living alone
It fulfills her maternal needs.
To greet her when returning home
To nurture, to pamper, to feed.

The dog is a family protector
He barks and growls when strangers appear
Guards the family as they sleep
To alert when danger is near.

The dog is a family protector
He barks and growls when strangers appear
Guards the family as they sleep
To alert when danger is near.

For a family like ours cog of a wheel
He belongs to one and all
It matters not how we treat him or feel
He's still at our beck and call.

I have written about the noble dog
And the cat who is loved so much
But what do we need of our feathered birds
Or a turtle or lizard or such?

When a child can't go to the ocean
The ocean can come to him.
He can dream of adventure, brawls at sea
While watching the fishes swim.

He'll wonder how a turtle can move
While wearing is house as a coat,
And how he can live both on land and sea,
How a duck can stay afloat.

A bird in a cage is wonderful sight
Or to hold it in one's hand.
The beauty we see as it flutters its wings
Is an art not created by man.

We wonder how it can fly so high
And not fall to earth as a stone
Because of questions such as these
Inventors build birds of their own

Well now is the time to tell
Of this family's pets galore
Of how they played a part in our lives
With compassion understanding and more

The first of our pets was a puppy named 'midge'
She was killed when struck by a car
And then came 'Boots' a cockered mutt
Whose mind wasn't quite up to par

Next a collie named 'Prince' who we couldn't keep
Who constantly ran away.
Then a huge black retriever named 'Blackie'
Showed up in a storm one day.

Blackie jumped fences, loved children,
And retrieved everything that he could.
Such as newspapers, boots, and garbage,
From all over the neighborhood.

But the day he saved our baby son
Was his greatest retrieve by far
He grabbed him by the seat of his pants
From in front of a speeding car.

Yes, but for this beautiful creature
Our Bud wouldn't be here today.
Blackie never know how grateful we were
I wish we could thank him some way.

He never belonged to anyone
Just to himself alone
So he chose to leave us one stormy night
To other parts unknown.

Then a cat named 'Pat' and a dog named 'Mike'
Were next to move into our hearts
But mostly they loved each other
They were seldom ever apart

Pat was a grey striped alley type
And Mike was an English setter
Pat ran away as cats will do
And Mike found a home that was better.

Then we said "No more dogs, no more cats"
We said "Emphatically Nope!"
But they knew we'd give in when Bud came home
With a pup on the end of a rope.

This pup became a very dear friend.
A black and tan setter named 'Rusty'
He watched our babies and loved the kids
And was always dirty and dusty.

Though he tracked up my kitchen and messed up the house
I loved him as much as they
Then years went by and age took it toll
And death took our Rusty away.

I forgot to mention that one Christmas
Eve We brought the children a kitten
A little fuzz ball all silver and white
One look and our hearts were all smitten

He turned out to be a cantankerous
Tom A meaner cat wasn't known
He gave our Rusty a terrible time
And soon began to roam

Between cat fights and buck shot his wounds wouldn't heal
So I know we must say goodbye
To the last of our cats, he was sent to rest
To the 'Pet Haven in the sky'

Well, by now we knew our footed friends
In our lives had a definite place
So after a family talk, we chose
A pup with a lovable face.

A cute little female beagle
Who gave us both laughter and tears
She became so much a part of our lives
She was with us eleven short years.

We chose to call her 'Snoopy'
(though she never came when called)
She could track and snuff out anything
Even creatures very small.

Then the 'Hunters' took her hunting
And she sniffed and flushed their prey
But when she heard the gunshot
She was frightened and ran away.

Though this ended her role as hunter
The retriever in her remained
She would bring an injured bird to me
That something else had maimed.

She would stay by its side till its wounds were healed
And she knew that it could fly
Then she'd watch it soar when we turned it free
And we knew she was saying goodbye.

She was tolerant of the pets we had
And was willing to guard them all
We had hamsters, and gerbils, lizards and turtles
All creatures large and small

Then Phil brought home a white rabbit
And she willingly shared her domain
They slept and played together
And closest friends became.

We have so many memories
Of her loyalties, friendships and strife.
Of the heroine in her that saved our
Pat From the bees that near took her life.

Of the puppies she bore, five litters in all
Of her comical laughable ways
How she'd run away, wouldn't come when called
And the games with a stick she would play

The, alas, one terrible evening
She was struck while chasing a car
She was lost in the woods, we searched and searched
Then gave up when it was dark

With heavy hearts and all hope gone
We thought of her out there alone
Then with great surprise, heard a whimper
She had dragged her injured self-home

With a broken back that would not heal
We knew just what we must do
The doctor head to put her to sleep
The merciful way, it's true

The family was saddened, we'd lost a friend
And of her our memories remain
She never really asked us for much
Just food and a warm place to stay.

Then the kids remembered a quote from
Dad and bought him a Father's Day gift.
The gift was an Airedale puppy
That gave our spirits a lift.

'Sir Rusty hinges' became his name
And a happier pet wasn't known
He looked like a big stuffed animal
Even when that he is grown.

Ah! Rusty, Ah! Rusty our lovable clown
Full of antics and play
You couldn't feel sad when he was around
With his funny, comical ways

He loved wearing hats, and chasing cats
And fuzzy tennis balls
He loved to frighten the paper boy
And the mailman most of all

Ah! Yes there are things that frightened him
Such as the kitchen floor
It took a lot of courage
To scamper from the door to door

And some of the things he loved the most
Are swimming in the lake
Running free in the country
And talking walks through the woods we would take

I can't say Rusty disliked birds
Though he just didn't show much love
He tolerated all the wild ones
But hated Pat's magical doves.

I guess, it's more like jealousy
Of the attention the doves received
A magician must train and care for his birds
If the audience he's to please

The doves, too, were part of our family
He had pink, yellow, blue ones and white
And when he produced them from nowhere
They were quite a beautiful sight

Well they too needed care as our Rusty did
(Pat paid for the birds as planned)
But the cost of the animal doctors,
And protection the law demands

And because of the kind of dog he is
His grooming costs seemed immense
We were on a very low budget
And we must cut out this expense.

So I looked at him and said to myself
'I know I would, if I could
I must learn the skill of grooming
Yes, I should, and I could and I would'

So with clippers in hand I worked in a shop
Till I learned all I needed to know
I went on to become a 'Dog Groomer'
And our income began to grow

It didn't grow by leaps and bound,
Enough to just get us by.
it helped with some of the extras
It bought up cookies and pie

If it hadn't been for this shaggy dog
I wouldn't have gained this skill
It's something I really liked to do
A particular need to fulfill

Yes, animals do play a major part
In the average family life
For when were sad, unhappy
And our life is full of strife

A dog by our side with a head to stroke
And warm brown, adoring eyes
Will tell you he loves you most of all
And some where there's blue skies.

Measure of a Man

What is the measure of a man?
 Not what you are today,
But, the distance you have traveled
 to become this certain way!

The stumbling blocks, the foolish things,
 the thoughtless things you do.
The mistakes you have corrected
 help to show you what is true!

The wayward trips along life's path,
 to fall to rise again,
makes you a little taller
 in the eyes of man!

It's not how far you have to go,
 but, where you're traveled from,
The things you've learned, strength you've gained
 may be the total sum!

It's what's inside, how far you reach
 to lend a helping hand.
These are the ways to know
 the measure of a man!!

(c) 1982

Mountain of a Man

I met a man when I was just a youth.
A time when I was troubled, searching for the truth.

Reckless times, not caring what I did or where.
Life didn't have a purpose, I simply didn't care.

I tried most everything, new things that came along.
It really didn't matter if it was right or wrong.

I searched for answers in smoke rings in the air,
In the bottom of a bottle, but the answers were not there.

Then one day I saw him, this mountain of a man.
He looked at me and smiled and took me by the hand.

He became a friend, a someone I could turn to when in need.
Someone I could talk to, I could follow, he could lead.

He helped me through those troubled times, this mountain
of a man.
I shall all my life be grateful, for he took me by the hand.

I'd like to place a statue in a park, so he'd be known,
A Harley Davidson with a rider, of marble or of stone.

It would tower there so proudly, with one extended hand.
Yes, there ought to be a tribute to this mountain of a man!

(c) 1982

Muse; Musings

My muse has left me, gone astray.
Perhaps I'll write another day.

Poetic words have taken flight;
All thoughts of rhyme clear out of sight.

But I'll not worry, I'll not fret.
It's never left for long, as yet.

I'll simply wait unit the day
When I can write my heart away.

My Children Taught
Me How to See

My children taught me how to see
        the beauty all around.
They taught me how to look beyond
        the surface of the ground,

We watched the honey-bees collecting
        nectar for their hives,
and busy little ants were trying
        just to stay alive.

They brought a tiny bird to me;
        it had an injured wing.
With nourishment and care we
        set it free to fly and sing.

We watched a spider spin its lacy
        web so skillfully,
and the beauty of a sunset
        nature painted artfully.

A Luna Moth, with folded wings,
        emerged from its cocoon.
With wings unfurled and color bright
        it wafted 'cross the moon.

Then when the daylight slowly
  faded into night,
the brilliant sky with all its stars
  became an awesome sight.

My children taught me how to see,
  took me gently by the hand,
taught me how to see the wondrous
  beauty of the lands

    (c) 1992

Mystery Of Migration

How does a bird know where to go
     Before the frost is on the ground?
How does he know which way to fly?
     Are there visible signs around?

How does he know which way is south?
     Can he tell East and West from North?
Is there a compass in his head
     To direct him where to go forth?

I wonder how those fragile wings
     Can carry him so far and long.
He still takes time along the way
     To brighten our day with a song.

When he returns in the springtime
     Is his home the same place each year?
How does he know his own specie
     When the opposite sex is near?

Some questions still go unanswered,
     Beyond the scope of mortal man.
The bird is of God's creations,
     Important to the Master's plan!

(c) 1984

New Beginning

I had not worked for thirty years,
financial status causing fears.
What should I do?
What could I do?
My lack of skills was very clear.

To baby-sit had no appeal,
to clean a house or cook a meal.
A paper route?
I ruled it out,
nor was I one to wheel and deal.

My fingers walked through yellow pages,
with wishful thoughts of future wages.
A job with pay,
a phone call away,
prevailing needs and hope presages.

Day one, new job, on time as planned.
Complete instructions well in hand.
Facing my client
I looked compliant,
hoping she would understand.

As I smiled with all my charm,
she sank her fangs into my arm;
life's blood draining,
courage waning,
no need to speak of my alarm.

Yet on went I, completing duty.
Proud and happy... what a cutie;
White fur fluffy,
pink bows puffy,
my poodle stood in all her beauty.

(c) 1989

Night Flight

The large bird dips its wings,
piercing through the dark ebony sky,
leaving clouds behind.

Before us lies a wonderland of lights,
hiding all the ugliness
of daylight hours.

God reminds
beneath the surface
there is beauty.

(c) 1994

Nights to Remember

Halloween is many things,
To some of us remembering's;
Porch lights shine on faces smiling,
Trailing costumes so beguiling.
From one house then to another
Protected by an older brother.
Rustling leaves beneath our feet.
Carefully crossing well lit streets.
"Trick or treat," the children shout,
Laughter echoing all about.
Jack-o-Lanterns fierce and scary
sacks of goodies, too full to carry.
Then trudging home through dark of night
To check the loot in home's sweet light.
Daddy in his big arm chair,
Waiting patiently for his share.

But today REAL monsters scurry!
Tampering is our greatest worry!
Yet, if we cancel out these hours,
There'd be no memories such as ours.

(c) 1986

No Time

4:00 A.M. It's happening again!

I'm soaked with perspiration.
How much time do I have?
Shaking in desperation;
Hurry, hurry to the kitchen.

Sugar, sugar, must have sweets!
Orange juice with sugar in it,
Or any other sugared treats.
Waiting now to still the trembling.

At last relief, beat the odds.
A bout; of Hypoglycemia.
Thank you, thank you, thank you, God!
Until the next time around!

(c) 2003

Nutriment

(Triads)

I

What is the mongrel to the flea?
What is the flower to the bee?
What is my daily bread to me?
Food to sustain!

II

What is the text book to the eye?
What is the query to the try?
What is the answer to the why?
Food for the brain!

III

What is the laughter to the tear?
What is the comfort to the fear?
What is the foresight to see clear?
Food to contain!

(c) 1983

Oh Poetry!

Oh poetry, I hear your name;
You speak of love, you speak of pain.
You speak of peace, you speak of war
And tragic moments by the score.

You sing of nature; sun and moon
As heartstrings play a tender tune.
You sing of distant memories
And reach back for them tenderly,
Of bird-song at the break of day
And laughter from a child at play.
You bring me joy, you make me cry,
Provoking thoughts, I know not why.

Your words flow free or speak in rhyme.
Traditional forms reach back in time.
I hear your voice where e're I be.
I know your name, oh Poetry.

(c) 1990

Onward, Ever Onward

My mind goes racing swiftly
   Down the runway of my life.

Onward, ever onward to
   Its final destination,
As a snowball gains momentum
   Without doubt or reservation.

I have traveled many pathways,
   Crossed a bridge or two,
Climbed the highest mountain,
   As I was meant to do.

I have had some quiet moments,
   In which to meditate,
Made some quick decisions
   Without time to hesitate.

I have rocked my babies gently,
   Sung a quiet song,
Shouted out in protest
   Against things I felt were wrong.

I have been there for my loved ones,
Yet, have I filled my every role?
Have I done what was intended?
Accomplished every goal?

As the clock is winding downward,
My minds race with time;
Onward, ever onward
Toward the finish line.

(c) 1989

Other Side of the Hill

I vaulted over the fence,
grass was greener there,
searching, searching searching
for a place I longed to be.

I sauntered through the meadow
to the rising hill ahead,
scrambled up and over,
landing in a valley down below.
Searching, ever searching
for that place I longed to be.

I hurried through that valley
where a mountain kissed the sky,
to climb the mighty, rocky, steep incline.

I stood atop the high plateau,
and lo and behold I saw it,
what I'd been searching for,
nestled in the panorama far below.

Down the mountain,
across the valley,
over the rising hill,
I tip-toed through meadow,
and over the fence anew.

It stood in all its glory.
It had been there all along,
that little piece of heaven I call home!

(c) 1999

Our Great Lakes are Shrinking

Our Great Lakes are shrinking,
9adly to say.
The ozone layer is
drifting away
as sun's rays seep into
earth's atmosphere.
The green-belts replaced by
concrete, I fear.

No marshes for shorebirds,
fish can't survive;
spawning: grounds needed to
keep them alive.

Year by year---inch by inch
our Lake a are shrinking:
the earths greatest source of
water for drinking.

(c) 1990

Pains of War

I picture blood on the battlefield,
envision cloth that bound his wounds.
Sorrow's a heavy burden I wield.
Tears flow free ... I kneel by his tomb.

I was not there to ease his pain,
to hold his hand or wipe his brow,
To soothe him as a child again,
or just to be with him somehow.

Yet, She was there so long ago.
She watched them nail Him to a cross.
Her pain was just as great, I know.
She felt as I do at Her loss.

Each nail they drove into His hands
must have pierced Her heart as well.
She knelt there on that rocky land,
no words of comfort could She tell.

So She and I must kneel and pray,
that other sons may live once more
to see eternal peace one day,
and never know the pains of war.

(c) 1999

Parade of Seasons

Each season parades it's beauty and charm;
  green grass of summer,
    the scent of roses,
  autumn leaves,
    the picture transposes,
  winter, oh winter,
    it's blanket of snow,
  spring brings new life,
    all things start to grow.
The seasons go marching, arm and arm,
  and life goes on,
     and on,
     and on!

© 1989

Phenomena

We studied skulls of ancient man
as they passed from hand to hand.
We learned the facts and age of each,
millions of years beneath the sand.

But when I held the "Baby Taung"
that lived three million years ago,
(they said a child the age of six)
I did not want to let it go.

As I looked upon its jutting jaw,
my heartstrings tugged, I felt a bond.
I closed my eyes ... held it close,
reluctantly I passed it on.

In the darkness of that night
I saw the waters rushing down.
I dreamt about that ancient child,
saw her tiny body drown.

Then from the text book I discovered,
she'd drowned, indeed ... I shed a tear.
That child had touched my heart
across a span... three million years.

(c) 1994

Pink Rhubarb Pie

There it sits
on a cooling rack
with a light, golden crust,
steam rising from its center
of sweet, mouth-watering
filling so pink.

Tempting,
teasing,
tantalizing aroma
making my nostrils flare.
I must wait until it cools
I think.

With my fork in hand
and plate on the stand,
knife ready to cut,
I wait and I sigh.
As soon as it's cool
I'll be ready to taste
my pink rhubarb pie.

(c) 1988

Plants

They told me I should talk to my plants,
      if I want them to grow and grow,
But what do you say to a plant that
      A plant doesn't already know?

Well, I gave them plenty of water
      and the right amount of sun.
Then I said to my Philodendron
      "Are you having any fun?"

And I asked my hanging Begonia
      "Are you happy? What's new with you?"
On to my African Violets, I said
      "Are you feeling kind of blue?"

Then around the house I went,
      Each plant a word or two.
Soon, I thought "How very silly!
      I've better things to do!"

So I gathered them all together
      and I said it once and for all.
I said "Plants, you talk to each other,
      for I'm not at your beck and call!"

I don't know whether it was what I said,
or what they talked about,
But, they seem to be growing much better!
I guess I'll never find out!

(c) 1983

Prison Walls

My two birds share a single cage,
one bird large, the other small.
No prejudice
No bigotry
Though one is blue and one is grey,
to them it matters not at all.

They chirp and chatter happily,
sleep side by side from dark to dawn.
No hate
No fear
No thought of what lay there beyond,
no thought of times now here and gone.

Yet WE erect our prison walls,
invisible thou they may be.
We segregate
We perpetrate
We judge what we don't understand
and tell ourselves that we are free.

If we are free why do we see
our fellow-man in only black and white?
Can color blind
And open mind
remove the bars, tear down the walls,
live in peace and set the wrongs to right?

(c) 1992

101

Procrastination

Why worry today
      when tomorrow will do?
And why cut the grass?
      It's a waste of time to.
Don't mend the shingles
      when the sky is bright blue.
Unless there is rain,
      water will not come through.
You can't fix the roof
      when it's raining outside.
So just sit and wait,
      let tomorrow decide.

You don't have to work,
      let the other guy slave.
If you grow a beard
      there'll be no need to shave.
Why save your money?
      Hurry spend it today.
Tomorrow is still
      such a long way away.

It may not be worth
    the high price it will cost.
You can't recapture
    all the time you have lost.
Your grass will be long,
    and your roof will still leak.
Your money is spent,
    no employment to seek.
You'll wake up one morn
    with a heart full of fear,
    For today is gone
    and tomorrow is here!

        (c) 1984

Ramon

Grubby hands with arms outstretching.
Huge dark eyes, so sad and pleading.
Brown skin children begging coins.
Pockets Jingle ---Pleas succeeding.

As I passed out coins I saw him;
A small muchacho stood alone.
His chin thrust forward, head held high,
A youth with pride, his name Ramon.

Refusing coins, he shook his head,
He clutched a rag, a box of wood.
"I shine your shoes; I shine your shoes,"
Said small Ramon, "I shine them good."

On my feet were canvas sneakers.
I had no choice, I just said "No."
Wishing I had worn my leathers,
Wishing I could help this Nino'.

Yet as I watched him polish boots,
(although the boots were not my own)
I felt there was a ray of hope
For Mexico and small Ramon.

(c) 1987

Reigning Rulers

Reigning Rulers stand before us
Anxious to impart
Wars of knowledge,
Sharing facts and thoughts.

Performing artists in every sense:
Pacing, chalk in hand,
Gesturing to emphasize,
Holding our lives at bay.

And in the end, with grades in hand,
We walk away
Richer for the knowledge gained
From reigning rulers in their realm.

(c) 1992

Remember Me

In each of us there is a need,
A need to live, a need to be,
A need to know the written word,
A need to speak verbally.

To leave behind a memory,
If it be word or thought or deed,
To be a friend to someone near,
To plant an inspirational seed.

Perhaps to win, perhaps to lose
The battle that I face each day.
If it be choice or destiny
Then let it be, let come what may.

I will not walk this path again,
Although well-trodden it may be.
Let it be known that I was here,
For there is only one of me.

(c) 1987

Roundelay for Today

God has given me sight and sound
And freedom to use as I may.
I searched for beauty all around
      Today.

I stopped to watch the children play.
Their joyful laughter had no bound.
They smiled. I smiled, then walked away.

I heard a song-bird's voice resound
And watched, in flight, a bright Blue Jay.
Nothing equaled my home, I found
      Today.

(c) 1984

Sanctuary

I vaulted over the fence,
(grass was greener there) searching,
ever searching for a place I longed to be.

I sauntered through the meadow
to the rising hill ahead,
scrambled up and rolling over,
landed in a valley down below.
Searching, ever searching
for that place I longed to be.

I hurried through that valley
where a mountain kissed the sky,
scuttled up the mountain side,
reached the high plateau.
Arms outstretched I turned around,
looking down I saw it ⋯
what I'd been searching for;

Down the mountain ⋯
across the valley ⋯
over the rising hill ⋯
through the lush green meadow ⋯
over the fence again.
It stood in all its glory,
(It had been there all along,)
That little piece of heaven
I call home!

(c) 1999

Scotts Bluff

I travel along the Oregon Trail,
    for me a trip down memory lane.
I was here long ago at Mitchell Pass,
    a region known as Nebraska's Great Plains.

Here at the foothills of Scotts Bluff I pause;
    a majestic monument proud and still,
remembering a time when my love and I,
    together had climbed this very hill.

There, standing in awe, spellbound hand
    in hand after reaching the top of this rocky butte,
we gazed all around on that high plateau.
    The picture-card beauty striking us mute.

The geometrical farmlands below
    appeared to be like a patchwork quilt.
We saw sunlight dancing on fields of wheat
    and man-made structures so carefully built.

Yet standing there on that hilltop so high,
    history seemed to be in the making.
The farmers below toiled with blood and sweat.
    Machines were still a new undertaking.

I picture the wagon trains rolling by;
    the great migration of forty three.
Thousands of pioneers passing through
    searching for land they were told would be free.

Their goals were westward to Oregon.
        Some of the families were Washington bound
As they traveled along the Oregon Trail;
        a treacherous journey on rock-strewn ground.

Weary from their months of travel,
        some families remained on this barren soil,
Deciding to make their homes on these plains,
        with undying hope and a will to toil.

They constructed houses from blocks of sod,
        strengthened with twigs, roots and weeds.
Trees were few so were sparingly used.
        Buffalo chips were fuels for their needs.

Battling droughts and the grasshopper plagues,
        when crops were destroyed to begin anew,
a brave and courageous people were they,
        fighting the Indians; Cheyenne and Sioux

Now here am I retracing my steps,
        reliving moments of days long gone by.
Thoughtful I ponder my own heritage.
        Perhaps my ancestors stood here as I.

Yes, Nebraska is a valiant state.
        I'm proud to have come from those pioneers.
And although I must travel on again,
        my heart will remain on this bluff so dear!

c) 1985

Seasons of my Heart

We were children in the springtime, laughing carefree
        children romping through the meadow hand in hand.
        with the fragrant scent of clover in the air.

A busy time was summer, duty calls, building home
        raising children, planning future. and the
        spicy smell of lilacs fill the air.

Autumn is a time for us, leisure time, children grown.
        vacationing in the south with friends, and
        The pungent scents of marigolds fill the air.

Now the winter frost is in my hair. You are gone, I'm alone.
        But, I remember when; strolling hand in hand
        in the moonlight, with sweet smell of roses in the air.

(c) 2003

Shape Up

(Sestina)

You may exercise while standing
If you touch your toes while bending.
You may exercise while lying
If you use your legs like running.
You may touch your toes while sitting
But, don't touch your toes while jumping.

If you touch your toes while jumping
On your feet you won't be standing
And it's doubtful you'll be sitting.
In a cast you won't be bending.
In a cast you won't be running.
In a cast you will be lying.

You will simply just be lying
maybe dreaming you are jumping
In a lake, or maybe running
Or perhaps you'll dream of standing
On a dock with fish pole bending
Or just wishing you are sitting.

Make your plans while you are sitting
So you won't end up just lying.
You may touch your toes while bending.
You may use a rope while jumping.
Touch your toes while you are standing.
Once around the block while running.

Twice around the block while running.
Touch your toes while you are sitting.
Sway from side to side while standing.
Bend you knees while you are lying.
Always use a rope while jumping.
Stretch with care when you are bending.

One, two, three, four keep on bending.
Stand in place while you are running.
Never touch your toes while jumping.
Now breathe easy while you're sitting.
Take a moments rest while lying.
Then stretch tall when you are standing.

Bending makes you look good sitting.
Running tires you for lying.
Pride is jumping, record standing.

(c) 1984

113

She

She---
born to the old century,
bound by tradition;
women's submission
to customs and law,
she was tethered and bound.

She balked---
felt a need to be free; a
desire to soar,
a will to explore,
to share what she saw,
to express and relate what she found.

She shocked---
striving for equality,
she let it be known,
at first all alone,
then others took pause
joining the cause all around.

She succeeded
in the right to be free;
to vote, to be treated equally.
Yet reaching so far
for the attainable star
has she sacrificed her feminine crown?

(c) 1990

Shell Game

One morning when the tide was low,
Hoping that a wave would throw
A treasure, as I walked along the shore.

I gathered shells, the common kind.
Lying there for me to find,
And yet I kept on wishing for much more.

I knew there was a special one,
Just meant for me, 'twas more than fun;
This was a game the ocean liked to play.

Then at eventide once more,
I walked along just as before
Still searching for "my shell" along the way.

All at once, to my surprise,
Right before my very eyes,
A playful wave just tossed it at my feet.

I looked upon it where it sat,
Pretty? No, it was not that,
But somehow it had made my day complete.

Then as I cupped it in my hand,
Retracing footsteps in the sand,
I turned to whisper "Thank You" to the sea.

I researched for its name and then,
Discovered it was called a "pen"'
Perfect for a post such as me!

© 1987

Show-time

The stage is set
    the script is ready
        lights adjusted
           cameras steady
              lines are learned

must not ferret.
With stand-by signal
    a hush descends
        the crew awaits
           actors ready to pretend
              as music swells
the show begins.
Working together as a team
can fulfill a writer's dream.

@ 1991

Snowflakes Fell

(A Tripod)

Snowflakes fell,
Although the month was April,
Knowing spring would soon be on its way.
I'll remember when the Snowflakes fell.

(c) 1989

It's dismal and cold, the trees are bare.
The earth is covered with snow.
Nature covered it over with care.
It's time to rest, little creatures below.

(c) 2000

Nature's a lady, I am told;
Each season a fashion show.
She dresses in green, then red and gold.
She's dazzling in her gown of snow.

(c) 2000

Spring

(The Pensee)

Welcome
I say to spring,
A time for joy and beauty;
Flowers bloom, birds return singing
Of new beginnings, love abounds.

(c) 1989

Still-Life

I tried to draw a mountain
    As high as it would go.
I tried to draw a river,
    But my river didn't flow.
I decided on my river
    There ought to be a boat.
Yet when I finished sketching,
    It didn't seem to float.
Next I drew a willow tree,
    and all it did was weep.
It stood there by my river
    And my mountain, not so steep.
I put them all together
    Beneath a cloudy sky,
With a little bit of sunshine,
    Sneaking, peaking from on high.
When I propped it on my table,
    I saw much to my delight,
A scene emerge before me,
    A still and peaceful sight.

(c) 1987

Super-Heroes

Jeffrey sat with pencil in hand,
beginning a drawing, simple as planned.
It appeared to take form ... coming to life.
As Jeffrey drew
the character grew;
a super-hero ... a battle of strife.

The struggle continued, creation and boy,
Jeffrey with pencil, his hero-made ploy;
a paper person ... one with its mentor.
It captured my heart,
right from the start.
They lived in a land I could not enter.

Making believe in a make-believe world
fighting a dragon with banners unfurled,
one fought with pencil, the other with sword,
both being strong
righting the wrong,
escaping reality with nary a word.

Then came a voice disturbing his reverie,
forcing aside his moment of chivalry.
The rest of the day he did what was deemed.
Yet with fading light,
in the dead of night,
his super-hero returned as he dreamed.

(c) 1989

Symphonies

The difference in the dark from dawn
    Is not just in the sight.
The sounds around us everywhere
    Are shades of black and white:
The tap, tap, tap of the raindrops
    Gently on the window pane.
The forceful sound of a tidal wave
    In league with a hurricane.
The whisper of a summer breeze
    Playfully teasing all things,
The ever-threatening tornado
    And fear of destruction it brings.

The silent tires of a bicycle,
    The squalling wheels of a car.
The almost noiseless glider,
    The jet that is heard so far.
The rat-a-tat-tat of a jack hammer
    In search of a broken main.
The digging sound of a shovel or hoe
    As a farmer plants his grain.
The blasting of the guns at war
    The silence of death's aftermath.
The cheers when the war has ended
    The tears for war-time's wrath.

The silence of a kitten's paw,
　　The heavy foot of a horse.
The tenderness of a lullaby
　　The opera singer, of course.
The cry of a hungry baby,
　　The contented coo when he's fed.
The shriek of children playing,
　　The sleeping child in his bed.
The crescendo of a heartbeat
　　Pounding when in fear,
The quiet, steady beating heart
　　Is like music to the ear!

(c) 1984

Tears

Tears are shed for many reasons;
For beauty of the changing seasons,
      seasons of the changing heart,
      time when we must be apart,
for heartfelt moments overflowing
with pride and joy of children growing.

When heartbreak fills us to the brim
and life seems hopeless ... even grim,
a hearty laugh from something funny
makes the world seem bright and sunny.
      Teardrop cloudbursts form release
      bringing forth an inner peace.

(c) 1990

Tell me Where

Where have you gone, little baby? The baby
I cuddled and kissed.
When did the lullabies vanish?
Where are the years I have missed?

Where have you gone, little lady?
Your dollies, bears, ribbons and bows,
are gone like the tea parties shared.
Those joy filled days.
where did they go?

Where have you gone little 'tween,
with pigtails and cap askew?
With dirty sneakers, grubby jeans,
where is the tomboy I knew?

Now you're a teenager, a woman/child,
like a thorn in my side, a prickly pear.
Soon you'll move on to another life,
Soon you'll be gone ... tell me where!

(c) 1999

Tempie in the Sky

I've longed to sit upon a mountain top,
and write about the vision I would see.
To grasp a bit of stardust in my hand,
and you my love, would be there next to me.

At first we would not feel the need to speak,
just sit there in the midst of all this wonder.
Absorbing all this magnitude of beauty;
a temple that no one should put asunder.,

The space around us vast, immense and pure,
free from smog and man's inventive fumes.
a breeze, a gentle kiss upon my face
removing every trace of earthly gloom.

Stars so bright I Id pluck one from the sky.
I'd hold it, careful not to mar its glow.
Then quickly I'd replace it in the heavens,
so it could light a pathway down below.

We'd sit there through the night until the dawn,
watch the sun rise slowly o'er the hill,
feel the gentle touch of morning dew,
and greet the painted dawn in silence still ·.

Slowly we would rise to flex our limbs,
our arms on stretched, our minds in thoughtful
prayer.
As Eagles fly, so would our- spirits soar
on wings of love, free from worldly care.

Trouble then would simply seem to fade,
drifting off with mystic clouds on high.
Still we would not feel the need to speak,
enfolded in God's Temple in the sky.

(c) 1986

Tercets

Dawn rudely pushed back the night.
The sun intruded with a golden light,
bringing with it a glorious sight.

The sun promised another hot day,
A chance to while the time away
through clouds above of puffy grey.

The shadows grow long and tall,
proclaiming, soon, night must fall.
I listen to the night birds call.

(c) 2003

Texas Turmoil

Stepping into the hot-tub, he noticed a string
attached to the button that would cause agitation.
He reached for the twine, it began to wriggle;
a snake he decided upon close observation.
With a twist of the wrist, a thrust of the hand,
he removed the serpent from his wet domain.
As he watched the invader coiling to strike,
its diamond-back colors gave clue to its name.
In awe he observed fangs ready for action.
(trapped ... he wondered if he should take flight)
Instead he approached it with weapon in hand,
removing the creature clear out of sight!

As time went by the story's retelling
became taller than tall, more daring and reckless.
The diamond-back rattler grew larger than large;
which isn't surprising, for it happened in Texas.

(c) 1989

The Birth of a Poem

In the beginning there's inspiration
Then the moment of inclination
Gathering tools for preparation
A transfer of thoughts to word formation
Rhythm and rhyme causing consternation
Must not forget the punctuation

A coffee break for restoration

Now back to work with expectation
It comes together with concentration
Words and thoughts without separation
A pause to dream of publication
Read it again with anticipation
At last it's finished ... a revelation

Behold! The birth of a poem.

(c) 1988

The Dance

I strolled along a well-trod path
One sunny afternoon.
      I didn't seem to have a care.
      The sound of birdsong filled the air.
I felt all nature was in tune.

I ambled on the twisted trail,
Not knowing just how far I'd gone.
      It seemed of time I'd lost all track.
      I thought, perhaps, I should turn back.
I realized how tired I'd become.

I stopped to rest upon a stump
Enjoying nature's wonderland.
      I felt a sudden urge to dance.
      My feet began to hop and prance.
My gesturing was wild and grand.

A lazy cow watched me perform,
Observing flailing arms and hands;
      A dance of creativity,
      Born of sheer necessity,
Fire-ants were crawling up my pants.

(c) 1993

The Goodnight Kiss

The goodnight kiss brings
comfort through the night,

Chases fears and troubles
far away,

Offers pleasant dreams
and happy thoughts,

Promising fulfillment
of a bright new day.

(c) 1994

The Legend of Finnegan's Farm

The long, sprawling ranch house
stood desolate, lonely, yet
eerily threatening.
The legend of Finnegan's Farm,
rumored to be evil incarnate!

Two lovers approached cautiously,
unaware of the legend or
what lay ahead. Stranded.
Nowhere to go.

The fire lit, they clung together,
warding off the chill,
the chill of the house,
the chill of fear.

It began with a moan, a groan,
a SCREAM!
Who was it?
What was it?
Upon exploration, no clues.
A skeleton in the closet!'

Then the aura surrounded them.
They tried to leave, but no escape!
Invisible walls held them captive.
Hours, days, nights,
no food, no way out,
only the sound of moaning,
groaning driving them to
madness!

Finally, all hope gone,
the lovers clung to each other
in death!

The Sea Gulls Gather

The Sea Gulls gather along the shore
In groups of, sometimes, ten or more.
A gossipy flock they seem to be,
Having their morning cup-of-sea.

A meeting of sorts; they complain and fuss,
Perhaps about mortals such as us,
Or maybe talking about their spouses,
Or how to improve their neighbors' houses.

Suddenly with a raucous cry
They flap their wings and take to the sky,
Dipping, soaring, swooping, skimming,
Wading the surf, rarely swimming.

Then after a long and tedious day
Of searching for food the usual way,
One by one they circle and land,
Wading and waiting as though it were planned.

The Sea Gulls gather along the shore
In groups of, sometimes twenty or more.
Another meeting it seems to me,
Having their evening cup-of-sea.

(c) 1988

The Silent Intruder

It crept into my home,
Silent,
Without warning,
Slowly
Overtaking everything
It could reach
On the lower level.

In past years
I was prepared
For the wet, murky culprit
That crept into my home,
But not so this time.

When the guardians
At their posts
Discovered
This intrusion,
The pumps
Were put into action.
Too late!

(c) 1987

Then and Now

Time moves slowly when we're young,
New horizons, songs unsung,
Bright new dawns, eager to play,
New discoveries every day.

Seeking adventure, friends to share.
Each new day without a care.
First as children, then as youth,
Searching eagerly for the truth.

Mid-life with its sadness and joys,
Buying more expensive toys.
Burdens to carry, goals to reach,
More money to earn, less to keep.

The golden years, the senior years,
Aging process bringing new fears.
Yet free to travel, free to choose
our way of life, win or lose.

If we could go back to yesterday,
Carefree days of frolic and play,
Would we change, or be the same?
Would old mistakes be made again?

(c) 1998

Time

What is time? Just a blink of an eye.
A second, a minute, an hour goes by.
A day, a week, a month and a year,
the past is gone, the now is here.

Time is an imp, an artful dodger,
A brand new babe, a very old codger,
an instant, a moment, a flash in the pan.
Sometimes it seems it's catch as catch can.

A clock counts the minutes now as I speak.
A calendar measures the days of the week.
Each month hand in hand with seasons portray
a portion of year in it's finest array.

Time is so precious, yet what do we do?
We take it, waste it and borrow it, too.
We're in it, we're on it, it's your time and mine.
We lose it or gain it by crossing a line.

However

I'll now end this poem, mere thoughts in rhyme,
For I ran out of word, and I'm all out of time!

(c) 1986

To The Fair

Grandma takes her pretty quilts, Grandpa takes his yams.
Mama takes her pickled pears. And Papa takes his lambs.
But I don't have a single thing to enter at the fair,
Cause I'm too little ...
I'm too young ...
Not old enough to share.

Yet, I can ride the Ferris Wheel (the little one, of course)
And I can ride the carrousel
(I have a favorite horse)
And I can watch the animals,
The cows and pigs are there.
I'm not too little....
Not too young...
I'm going to the fair.

(c) 1990

Travels End

At last I'm home,
So weary and glad.
Happy to be here,
Yet I am sad.

    I waited and waited
    With anticipation.
    I carefully planned
    This glorious vacation.

        It's over so quickly,
        with the fleeting of time.
        Though my travels have ended,
        The memories are mine.

        (c) 1985

Treasure Trap

Dreams of wealth above comprehension
Fulfilled/shattered beyond expectation.

Row upon row the 'bandits' await
while players pull levers ... anticipate.

The spinning wheels, the flashing lights,
the clinking of coins fill the room with delight.

With the toss of the dice, caution is lost,
yet hope for the 'big one' at any cost.

The lights on the 'strip' turn night into day,
and millions change hands as the gamblers play.

(c) 1992

Tree-Top Angel

Little angel on top of our tree,
     so high up there, will you watch over me?
Will you spread your wings as if in flight;
     surround us with your golden light?
Will you be our guardian, night and day,
     all through this blessed holiday?

Do you get weary up there so high?
     Sometimes I think I hear you sigh.
I saw you in a dream one night,
     so lovely, fragile, misty white.
You sang as only an angel sings,
     accompanied by the hum of your wings.

I know you get lonely and curious, too,
     especially when there's no gift for you.
Well this year there will be, wait and see;
     a special package beneath the tree.
A gift for you, all shiny and bright,
     wrapped in stardust, there in plain sight.
A tiny prayer, and a lot of love,
     to take with you to heaven above.

But, when Christmas is over, angel dear,
I must pack you away for another year.

(c) 1988

143

Tummy's are In

Man or woman
    Short or tall
        Rich or poor
            One and all
I've observed folks everywhere---
    Tummy's are in!

Run a little
    Exercise
        Tone your biceps
            Firm you thighs
Eat correctly—don't despair—
    Tummy's are in!

Do not slouch
    Stand tall and strong
        Move that pouch
            Where it belongs
In the foreground—it's the trend—
    Tummy's are in!

Tuck in in
    Or hang it out
        Makes no difference
            Look about
You'll be in fashion in the end—
    Tummy's are in!

(c) 1990

Thirty One-Untitles Poems

ANGELS ARE SHAKING THEIR PILLOWS;
THE SNOW IS BEGINNING TO FALL.
IN TIME FOR THE CHRISTMAS SEASON.
LET'S ENJOY IT, ONE AND ALL.

BELLS -- BELLS -- BELLS -- BELLS.
REMINDING US THAT ALL'S NOT WELL.
THERE ARE HUNGRY CHILDREN IN THE STREETS.
A COIN OR TWO WILL HELP THEM EAT.

CHURCHBELLS RING, WHAT DO THEY SAY?
COME INSIDE TO KNEEL AND PRAY.
JOIN US, FOR A CHILD IS BORN!
WELCOME HIM THIS CHRISTMAS MORN.

Have you seen the stranger who follows me?
He is tall black and thin as can be.
I turn around,
He's on the ground.
A very evasive fellow is he!

With love in your heart,
God in your soul,
A prayer on your lips every day;
With a smile on your face,
Though troubles prevail,
You problems will fade away.

I have a friend, who is always on call,
He patiently sits and waits in the hall.
Sometimes he's still.
Sometimes he's shrill.
Though he talks he hasn't a mind at all.

Nature's a lady, I am told.
Each season is a fashion show.
She dresses in green, then red and gold.
She's dazzling in her gown of snow.

Cook the meal, clean the house.
Let a trap to catch that mouse.
Change the babe, mend a seam.
Would you call this a housewife's dream?

Did you ever notice a rose-bud,
So slender in a vase?
She slowly opens her petals,
To show her beautiful face.

Assembling a simple object
That even a child can do,
Is a task no meant for grown-up.
Especially for me and you!

It's dismal and cold, the trees are bare,
The earth is covered with snow.
Nature covered it over with care.
It's time to rest, little creatures below.

Lovely lady dressed in blue.
I have a special place for you.
In my home and in my heart.
We're never very far apart

They nailed this gently man
To a rugged, wooden cross,
The sky was darkened, raindrops fell.
The heavens thundered at the loss.

Once each year we take the time
For a giant shopping spree.
Send Christmas cards with words that rhyme,
And decorate a tree!

Houseplants fill my barren walls.
They bring the outdoors in.
On a dismal, dreary morning
They help my day begin.

Whether the weather be rain or shine,
A variety of people will be there.
Some just browsing, some will buy
From the artists displaying their wares.

No need to drive for miles and miles
To enjoy the autumn hues.
Just gazing up and down my street
I see spectacular views!

I watch the wild geese in the sky
They fly in perfect formation.
Just as an arrow shooting forth,
On course to its destination.

Angels are shaking their pillows;
The snow is beginning to fall.
In time for the Christmas season,
Let's enjoy it, on and all.

Bells—bells—bells—bells.
Reminding us that all's not well.
There are hungry children in the streets.
A coin or two will help them eat.

Church bells ring, what do they say?
Come inside to kneel and pray.
Join us, for a Child is born,
Welcome Him this Christmas morn.

The old man said to the infant, new,
"We've something in common, me and you.
I'm almost bald, your hair is thin.
We both have a very toothless grin."

"Tramp, tramp, tramp" say the marching feet
On a busy shopping day.
The army of people move down the street,
With Christmas not far away.

A dog to a boy is a wonderful toy.
A remarkable combination!
Unless he's reminded, somehow this boy
Will forget his obligation.

Hurry, get ready! Tommy's waiting!
A glance in the mirror, anticipating.
I must look nice, we;re going to park
At the drive-in movie, in the dark!

What is time? Just a blink of an eye!
The seconds, the minutes, the hours go by.
The past is gone, the now is here.
What comes next is never quite clear.

Mirror, mirror on the wall,
Who's the prettiest on of all?
Her husband said it must be she.
Say's she "Love's blind, he can't mean me!"

Poor mother cat, she has no home!
With her kitten she must roam.
Hopefully someone will take pity,
Open a door for her and her kitty.

Footsteps echo in the hall.
Ignore graffiti on the wall.
School isn't what it used to be!
Or is it erased from my memory!

There are those who have so little to eat.
There are those with affluence.
Is there anyway the twain can meet,
So the scales will somehow balance?

No matter how far I wander,
No matter how far I roam,
The bathroom will still be untidy
When I return to my home.

(c) 1984

Vessels

If I were a teapot I'd fill a cup,
     but I'd save a cupful with care.
Someone may visit and pick me up
     then I'd have something to share.

If I were a chimney I'd send out smoke
     when the firelight dances about.
Without me the air would surely choke,
     and the fire would quickly go out.

If I were a well, with a pump above,
     I would never let me go dry.
I'd offer my cool, cool water, with love,
     to anyone passing nearby.

Though I'm not a teapot, chimney or well,
     I am like a vessel, of course.
My mind a container of thoughts to tell;
     emotions, love, fear and remorse.

I hope my vessel holds thoughts and words
     as pure as a drink from a well.
That what I say is worth being heard.
     and my doubts and fears will dispel.

Though I'm not a teapot, I'd like to share
        a cupful of cheer now and then.
I'd like to give comfort, here and there.
        Again, again and again.

And may my vessel have space to consume
        ideas for use, new and old.
May I, like the chimney, release the fumes
        so my heart may never grow cold.

(c) 1983

Waiting

The floor boards creaked loudly in the old weathered shack.
The wind whistled softly through the window cracks.
The pump squeaked and squealed from the ancient well,
and the house had more stories than it cared to tell.

The tumble-down barn and the shed worn and weary stood
near the stable, long empty and dreary.
The old whiskered man by the firelight's glow,
sat rocking and dreaming of days long ago,
remembering times when his house was a home.
With his wife by his side, he was never alone.
There were times when he walked with his mule and his
plow,
when daybreak would find him out milking the cow.
After planting the seed, the corn would grow tall,
and the peas and the beans were the best crops of all.

Now he sat there alone, as though waiting in line,
waiting to join her in a new life and time.
With the first light of dawn, a smile on his face,
he arose from his chair, felt her loving embrace.
Through the unopened door they walked hand in hand
to a glorious future, to a promised land.

c) 1991

What If

One morning the sun didn't shine,
the earth lay in darkness all day long?
What if the rain forgot to rain
and the songbirds forgot their song?

What if the moon didn't light the night
and the stars forgot to glow?
What if the oceans stopped to rest
the wind forgot to blow?

What if the lakes and streams dried up,
and the fishes died in the sea;
no water to drink, no food to eat,
then all creatures would cease to be.

There wouldn't be spring,
there wouldn't be fall,
there wouldn't be any
seasons at all.

If that should happen,
sad but true,
There wouldn't be me
and there wouldn't be you.

(c) 1993

What Then

The whole world awaits with bated breath
    The approach of the new millennium.
        Out with the old, in with the new
            We know not what to expect.

Time marching on day after day,
    Week after week, month after month until
        Out with the old, in with the new
            In the blink of an eye...what then?

(c) 1999

What's in a Name

What's in a
   name,
  a name a
   name?
   Shakespeare said
    a rose is the same.

    If Gwen wasn't Gwen
     or Ann was Fran,
      if Rachelle was Nell
     and Joe was Dan,

      If Don was John,
      Nancy was Betty,
      If Jan was Sarah,
       and Jean was Hattie,

If Marge
  was Polly
   and Danitza
   was Holly,

,

    If Linda was Sue,
     and Gerry was Jenny,
      or if Tom was known
     as Lenny or Benny,

If Esther was Carol,
and Judy was Mary,
if Ellen was known
as Sherri McClary

Then what about me,
if my name was Mame?
would I be different,
or be the same?

It wouldn't matter because in the end,
A rose is a rose, and we'd still be friends.

(c) 1993

Who Knows?

As they were saying their goodbyes,
My back was turned, I did not see
The flash of light that sped across the sky.

They pointed upward shouting, "UFO!"
"A UFO"... skeptically I jeered,
"And yet," I thought ... "who knows?"

(c) 1994

Wisdom

Oh, little did I know what I should know,
For school was unimportant to me then.
I did not value learning long ago.
If I could turn the clock back one again,
I'd grasp each learning moment by the tail.
To every written word I'd hold on tight.
I'd read and write and study without fail,
from early morn and far into the night.
I'd be a book of knowledge self-contained,
Remembering each thing I ever read,
and then I'd put to use what I'd retained,
to make a better world before I'm dead.
As children we pretend, anticipate,
But wisdom comes with age, sometimes too late!

(c) 1986

Woman's Fate

It's woman's fate
To weep and wait
While men go off to war.

Its woman's way
To kneel and pray
Till they return once more.

If woman's fears
And woman's tears
Could wash away the hate

A woman's hand
Could calm the land
And peace would emulate.

(c) 1988

Words

Words fall lightly from my mind
forming thoughts I would impart.
Yet words alone cannot not define
the depth of love within my heart.

(c) 1995

Song lyrics

By Dorothy

Dreaming of You
He's Always There

Dreaming of You

(song lyric)

Twilight descends and shadows fall.
    A glint of golden memories call.
        Once again I find I'm dreaming of you.

In the stillness of the night,
    I long to hold you oh so tight,
        Remembering a melody once heard.

Chorus

    I'm so afraid to close my eyes,
    afraid that I'll find
    this lovely dream is just
    a silly illusion.

Daytime carries me along,
    enfolding me in duty's song.
        You are there in every thought and word.

When twilight closes out the day,
    I hear your voice, I hear you say,
        We'll meet again, I too,
            am dreaming of you."

(c) 1991

He's Always There

I have a friend, the greatest kind.
He fills my soul, my heart and mind.
I love Him and He's always there for me.

He shares my thoughts, my every dream.
although how foolish they may seem.
He understands, He's always there for me.

    Refrain:
             He listens to my every prayer.
             He understands, He's always there.
             He's always, always, always there for me.

I feel His presence everywhere;
A gentle touch, a breath of air,
I know within my heart He's there for me.

We walk together hand in hand,
the extra footprints in the sand.
I'm not alone, He's always there for me.

Refrain:
             I feel His presence everywhere.
             I'm not alone, He's always there.
             He's always, always, always there for me.

Then when I draw my final breath,
to cross the line from life to death,
I'm certain that He will be there for me.

When I awake to live once more,
pass through St. Peter's pearly door,
I know He will be waiting there for me.

Refrain:
> I know that He'll be waiting there for me.
> I know that He'll be waiting there for me.
> He's always, always, always there for me.

(c) 1994

Skits

By Dorothy

Puppet Clown
The Emigrants
Tribute To A Pine Tree

Puppet Clown

(A Skit)

Characters: Puppet Clown
                 Good Witch

Puppet: Center stage – head drooping – arms hanging
         Limply.

Witch: No dialogue – action only – walking around clown
         Looking puzzled – discovers string
          (real or Imaginary)
          (grasping it with an upward motion.)

Puppet begins to recite and perform.

Clown:
         I'm a clown, I'm a clown, I'm a clown,
         With a smile on my face, not a frown.
             (smiling and frowning)

         I can dance, I can sing, (dancing from side to side)
         When they pull my string (gesturing with thumb)
         I can make people laugh all around.

         It's not fair, it's not fair, it's not faire
             (Looking sad)
         For about me they really don't care. (Shaking head)

I'm not a girl, nor a boy,,
Just a clown, just a toy,
No it's not; no it's not really fair.

Oh I wish, how I wish, how I wish (clasping hands)
I could be a real person complete.
I would dance, I would sing (dancing from side to
side)
Without that old string, (gesturing with thumb)
Move my arms, my hands and my feet.
       (move arms and hands point to feet)

Witch will tap with wand – Puppet will come alive.

Puppet:
       I'm alive, like you and like you. (Looking happy)
       I feel like a person, brand new!
       I can shout "Trick or Treat"
              (Cup hands to mouth as if to shout)
       To the people I meet, pretending like other kids do.

Puppet:
       Look at me, look at me, can't you see?
       I have candy and popcorn to treat.
              (Pretend to pull treats from bag)

       I can laugh, I can shout, with my friends all about.
              (Gesture to friends in audience)
       And I'm careful when crossing the street.
              (Leaning forward to indicate importance of
              Being careful when crossing a street.)

       When it's over, no more, no more, (looking sad)
       I'll be tossed with the toys out of sight.

I'll be happy, not sad,
　　　(Changing expression from sad to happy)
With the memories I've had
Of this wonderful Halloween night.

Witch and clown more forward with exaggerated bow.

(c) 1990

The Emigrants

(A one Act play)

By

Dorothy A. McIlvenna

The Emigrants

Cast of Characters:

Papa

Mama

Grandma

Meg:　　　*A girl about age 10*

John:　　　*A boy about age 9*

Georgie:　　*A boy about age 8*

Time: about the year 1895

Place: A shabby room in a small house somewhere in Europe.

Synopsis:	The scene opens on a shabby room. The family has just completed preparations for their long journey. They are emigrating to America. Grandma is seated on one of three old wooden chairs standing near the wall. Papa, Mama and the children are placing their bundles and bags of belongings near the doorway. Papa has just finished tying a rope around a large worn-looking suitcase. He places it next to the others. He straightens up looking around to make sure nothing has been forgotten. He walks toward the chairs.
Papa:	(stretching himself) "Well, we are at last ready to leave for America. Mama, come sit over here for a minute to rest." (Mama, walking across the room sits on one chair, Papa on the other. The children follow to kneel on the floor before them, Meg clutching a rag doll, the boys holding their caps) "Let us talk First we will ride the train to the place where the great ship is waiting to take us to the new land."
Mama:	"It is important that we stay close together, so that we so not become separated. It will be a very long journey."
John:	"Please, Papa, tell us again why we are going to America."

Papa: "We are going there to a better life for our family. It is difficult to make a living here, and the government is cruel to families like us. There are many opportunities in America. It is a land of freedom."

Georgie: "What will it be like when we get there, Papa?"

Mama: "Why don't we let Grandma tell us about it? She has been there for a visit."(All eyes turn to look at Grandma)

Grandma: "'It is a wonderful land where people can be free to do anything--to be anything they want to be--to go to any church they choose. It is a land of opportunity The first thing we will see when we enter the New York harbor is the Statue of Liberty. She is a beautiful lady. Meg has studied the words written on the statue. Meg, please tell us what they say."

Meg: (rising and moving to stand next to the piture of the statue on the wall. Meg begins to recite.) "Keep ancient land, your storied pomp! Give me your tired, your poor, Your huddled masses yearning to be breathe free. The wretched refuse of your teeming shore. Send these the homeless-tossed to me. I lift my golden lamp beside the golden door." (They were silent for a moment, then Meg knelt again.)

John:	"But Grandma, why did you not stay there when you were there?"
Grandma:	"Because I missed my family. I needed to be with you. (Gesturing to all of them) You are my family."
Georgie:[1]	"Tell us what it will be like on the ship, Papa. Will it be a very long journey?"
Papa:	"Yes, and it will be very crowded. Because we must be careful with our money, we will be down below in the of the ship they call Steerage. You will be allowed to go up on the deck now and then. Yes, it will take a very long time."
Meg:	"Where will we stay when we get there Will we have a very fine house?"
Mama:	"Papa has told me when we arrive in New York; we will find a place to stay. Papa will find a job, for he has many skills. I can earn money, by sewing or taking in washing. Even children in America can find jobs."

Papa: "But, of course, you must go to school. We will need to learn the language of America. When you go to school you can teach us all you have learned. When we have saved enough money we will go west where there is good farmland to be purchased. Then we will build a fine house. We will have chickens and cows and (smiling at the children) a dog to keep the cows from straying."

Grandma: "Don't worry, my children, it will be all right. We are a family!, and families are important. God will watch over us."

Papa: (with a sigh) "Well, it is time for us to leave." rise. Papa and the boys placing their caps on their heads--grandma drawing her shawl up to cover her head--Mama doing the same and helping Meg with hers, tying it under her chin, Meg still clutching her doll. (They walk toward the door, picking up their bundles--Papa picking up the large suitcase. They pause and turn for one last look--then exit)

Tribute To A Pine Tree

(A One Act Play)

By

Dorothy McIlvenna

Tribute To A Pine Tree

Act 1 – Scene 1
<u>Spring</u>

The curtains part, 'tis the first bud of spring.
The trees awaken from a long winter's nap,
Flexing their limbs that are stiff from the cold,
And feeling, within, the flow of the sap.

There's a bit of chill, dew on the grass.
A soft, gentle breeze has freshened the air.
A promise of summer not far away,
And violets, so why, peeking out with care.

A damp, musty odor of mulching leaves
Those have covered earth wet from melted snow.
Creatures, down deep, are beginning to stir
Because soil has thawed from the sun's warm glow.

Yet, all through the long winter's cold and snow
A sentry has stood, so green and so fine,
With feet planted firmly, still at his post.
There stands our hero the mighty pine!

Yes, there stands the Mighty Pine!

Act 1 - Scene 2
Summer

It's summer – there's a sweet harmony;
The chirping of birds, the buzz of the bees.
You listen – you hear a soft melody;
The rustling leaves from the warm, gentle breeze.

Most of the birds have returned from their flight,
Busily searching for just the right mate,
Preparing to nest in just the right tree.
Instinct has told them she right place and date.

The fruit trees have blossomed in full array.
The maple has formed her whirly bird seeds,
The willow is waving, welcoming all.
Beneath, a carpet of flowers and weeds.

Yet, nothing has changed from the tall pine tree.
Each season alert, he stands there waiting.
His thick, green foliage the same all year long.
His branches outstretched, anticipating.

Yes, there stand the Patient Pine!

<u>Act 1 – Scene 3</u>
<u>The Storm</u>

A thunderous roar heard in the background,
The forest is warned of approaching doom.
The beating drums become forceful and loud.
The sky is suddenly darkened with gloom!

With a crash of cymbals, lightning flashes,
Then a torrential downpour of rain.
The storm attacks with a sinister howl.
The forest is devastated with pain!

The woodland creatures run helter skelter,
Frightened they burrow, they hide from the storm.
Birds are frantically searching for shelter.
Their nest are flung to the winds, ripped and torn.

Yet, there stands a refuge, so tall and so staunch.
He beckons; he calls "come to me!"
The animals, birds snuggle close to him.
They know they are safe with the tall pine trees!

Yes, there stands the fearless Pine!

Act 1 – Scene 4
Aftermath

The maple tree's limbs are all torn apart.
The storm has destroyed the oak and the birch.
The willow tree weeps and the elm tree creaks.
The poplar tree bends and the sumacs lurch.

The aspen quakes, the apple tree shivers,
Flinging green apples all over the ground.
At last the terrible storm has subsided,
And it's suddenly silent all around.

Small woodland creatures peek out, one by one.
Cautiously they come out from their hiding.
The wings of the birds make a flapping sound,
Preparing to fly, chirping and chiding.

The woodland's a scene of mass destruction,
And the forest seems to whisper and whine.
Yet, through it all, so brave and so strong,
Still standing tall is the noble pine!

Yes, there stand the Nobel Pine!

Curtain Call

It's autumn – the forest has healed its wounds.
The trees are dressed in their finest display.
Small creatures are busily storing food,
And birds that must migrate have flown away.

The woodland alive with activity.
Nature reminding that winter is near.
They must be prepared for the snow and cold.
Yet, the forest is safe – they do not fear.

A shadow falls – then it brightens once more.
The trees in their glory wait for applause.
The birds make an entrance, tipping their wings.
The scampering animals stop to pause.

I look on in awe with my hands clasped tight.
I drink in, savor the beauty I see.
This curtain call is a breathtaking sight,
And there, center stage, stands the tall pin tree!

Yes, there stand the Might Pine!

(c) 1985

Essays

By
Dorothy

By the Dawn's Early Light

On a cold September morn on a warship in Chesapeake Bay, from the hands and mind of a poet, Frances Scott Key, our National Anthem was born.

It was during the War of 1812 that battles were being fought for freedom of the seas. The battle that concerned Francis Scott Key, a prominent lawyer in Washington, took place in the year of 1814 when the British fired on Fort McHenry which protected the city of Baltimore.

When Francis learned that his friend William Beanes had been captured by the British, he knew he must find a way to have the prisoner released. Joined by another attorney, John Skinner, they implored President James Madison to allow them to board the U.S. prisoner exchange ship where Beanes was being held. It was anchored at the rear of the British fleet. The vessel had been taken by the British when they had been run out of Washington. President Madison arranged for them to board and agreed to do what he could to support the cause.

As the two men boarded the vessel, they learned that not only would they be held prisoners, too, but that the warships were preparing to bombard Fort McHenry. It was September 13, 1814 and the battle raged all through the day and night. The fort had little defense. Francis and John paced the deck, chilled to the bone from the cold, bitter dampness of the misty sea air. From their vantage point they watched, in great frustration and sadness, the shelling of their countrymen. Even when dawn came they did not know who the victors were.

Suddenly, a break in the mist cleared the view and they saw the American Flag still flying over the walls of the fort.

Francis was so overcome with joy, he felt the need to express himself. He pulled an unfinished letter from his pocket and began to scribble verses. The words seemed to flow from the poet's fingertips:

"Oh, say can you see by the dawn's early light what so proudly we hailed at the twilight's last gleaming? Whose broad stripes and bright stars thro' the perilous fight, O'er the ramparts we watched were so gallantly streaming? And the rockets' red glare, the bombs bursting in air, Gave proof thro' the night that our flag was still there. Oh, say does that star-banqled banner vet wave O'er the land of the free and the home of the brave."

Later that day the three prisoners were released and Francis returned to Baltimore where he finished the other stanzas:

"On the shore dimly seen through the mist of the deep, Where the foe's haughty host in dead silence reposes, What is that which the breeze, o'er the towering steep, As it fitfully blows, half conceals, half discloses? Now it catches the gleam of the morning's first beam, In full glory reflected, now shines on the stream. 'tis the star-spangled banner. Oh, long may it wave O'er the land of the free and the home of the brave." "And where is that band that so vauntingly swore That the havoc of war and the battle's confusion, A home and a country should leave us no more? Their blood has washed out their foul footstep's pollution.

No refuge could save the hireling and slave, From the terror of flight or the gloom of the grave. And the star-bangled banner doth wave O'er the land of the free and the home of the brave."

Oh, thus be it ever when free men shall stand Between their loved home and the war's dissolution, Blest with vict'ry and peace, may the heav'n-rescued land Praise the Pow'r that hath made and preserved us a nation. Then conquer we must, when our cause it is just, And this be our Motto, "In God is our trust." And the star-spangled banner in triumph shall wave O'er the land of the free and the home of the brave."

The poem was printed on hand bills and distributed throughout the city. The tune that was added was taken from an old English drinking song. Ferdinand Durang was the first to sing the anthem in public. Three months later it was played during the Battle of New Orleans.

Friendly Competition

When you reach that certain age, sometime after retirement and when you find yourself spending more time at the doctor's office than you do at home, it is not unusual to compete with your peers.

For example: Sam and George, long time acquaintances, met at the credit union. Sam was standing in line, and George was about to leave having already completed his transaction. They greeted each other with a hearty handshake and proceeded to talk. Sam asked, "How are you, George?" The wrong thing to ask unless you really wanted to know or if you have a lot of time.

George answered, "Well, the old ticker ain't what it used to be." He then began to count off his ailments on his fingers, expounding on his many medical mishaps and miraculous recoveries.

When he paused for a breath Sam, who by this time had given up his place in line, interjected that he, too, was a walking miracle. Jamming his hands in the pockets of his brown suede jacket and shifting to a more comfortable position, began enumerating on his many operations and hospital stays. He needed to take eighteen pills a day to slay in moderately good health.

At this point, paunchy ruddy-faced George stretched himself to about an inch taller, stating he took twenty four pills a day. The conversation quickly turned to golf scores, more competition, other sports, hobbies, chores and ... their wives.

With women it is different, but competition none the less. When Sarah and Ann stumbled on to each other in the super-market one afternoon, the subject of their health was skimmed over lightly, moving on to compare notes about their children. Sarah had six grown children, all doing well, achieving executive levels in their chosen professions, having married well and living lives of model families. She had seven grandchildren and, of course, they were the most beautiful intelligent children on the face of the earth.

Ann, on the other hand, had only five children, but she had eight grandchildren. Their attributes were equal, if not superior, moving up a couple of steps on the hierarchy ladder.

When Sarah, with a twinkle in her eye, glorified in the announcement of a brand new great-grandchild, the conversation quickly turned to bingo, arts and crafts, gossip about mutual friends and ... their husbands.

They parted, after having sufficiently blocked the aisle with their shopping carts saying, "We must get together for lunch someday soon."

Competition is the spice of life. At this stage of life we need all the spice we can get!

Kicks On Route 66

U.S. Route 66, a 2,200 mile long four lane highway, Stretching from Chicago, Illinois to Santa Monica, California, Is the subject of controversy. It was an historical moment When it was completed, connecting the east to the west—Lake Michigan to the Pacific Ocean—a first of its kind and a Forerunner of our modern expressways.

An article written by Eric Zorn for the Chicago Tribune and appearing in last week's Detroit Free Press, expressed his feelings about the possible demise of this memorable highway, Referring to it as buzzard meat in Flagstaff, Arizona. He stated:

He basically said that In the last 30 years the remaining signs were taken down along the route. All the publicity and reminders from journalists finally subsided which put this no longer in the spot light of issues.

Even though the Government said there was no longer Route 66, the pavement and the community along the Route is still there as a reminder. The nostalgia of driving the 2,200 mile road cannot remove the real signs of the people. There is still a history of accomplishment of what the people did along this road. A community Of citizens that proved Route 66 did exist. We will still Celebrate what the people accomplished in history.

Jeff Meyers, Vice President of the association added, 'it's Hard to explain why, but 66 was unique in itself— it was 'The Grapes of Wrath,' it was people and legends and the characters." The organization has grown to 200 members and they hope to expand to other states along the route.

When first completed in 1926 the great highway spanned two-thirds of the country, an unbroken stretch from Chicago to Santa Monica, and proved to be the nation's most famous highway—a symbol of fun, freedom and escape. It was the only way to go from sun-loving vacationer—for Hollywood bound teenagers searching for stardom—for oldsters longing for a land of Orange groves, palm trees, and no more snow—for Americans with California on their minds. Yes, Route 66 was the only way to go.

We not only traveled on Route 66, but we exchanged stories and adventures about it, we rote script about it for a long running TV series entitled "Route 66 and we sang about it "Get your Kicks on Route 66""

"If you ever plan to motor west,
Travel my way, take the highway
That's the best.
Get your kick's on Route 66."
In an article by John M. Crewdson in The New York Times, he described the highway as follows:

Motorist who followed it through three time zones and eight states saw the verdant Missouri Ozarks and the dry brown plains of Oklahoma and the Texas Panhandle—the painted mesas of New Mexico and Arizona and the shimmering Mojave Desert—Hoover Dam and the Grand Canyon. Visitors from every state met and mingled in the road houses, tourist courts and diners were vivid contrasts of American speech, culture and geography were on display.

Big deal" you say? Well, it was a big deal because there were no connecting highways before that time. Slabs of concrete would run through the main streets of a city or town, but between the communities were mostly muddy, rutted or graveled roads. They were not kept up like they are today. It was up to the local residents and farmers to do so. Yes, it was a big deal.

> "it winds from Chicago to L.A.,
> More than 2,000 miles all the way. Get you kicks on Route 66."

Over the years, motels, gas stations, diners and shops selling curios from their respective locations, reflecting the coloration of the cities and stages through which double 6 passed, have been the main source of income for numerous small villages. Tucumcari, New Mexico is one such town with its 36 restaurants—58 service stations—and 48 motels. It has been deeply affected. The merchants there formed a group calling themselves the ant bypass Association in 1963, one year after President Eisenhower signed a law creating the 42,500 mile system of interstate highways, among them the ones that would replace Route 66; I-55 from Chicago to St. Louis, I-44 from St. Louis to Oklahoma City, I-40 the rest of the way. Tucumari has been fighting the issue ever since. They were assured that the new system would not affect them or cut them off, however, one morning the 7,000 residents were Awakened to the sound of silence—the new bypass had bypassed them without notice. The town has depended upon the motorist trade for their livelihood for about 35 years. It is sad to think that progress, so important to our nation, has to hurt the little folks.

> "Now you go through St. Louis,
> Joplin, Missouri—Oklahoma City
> Looks mighty pretty,
> You'll see Amarillo—Gallop, New Mexico,
> Flagstaff, Arizona.
> Don't forget Winon's, Kingman, Barstow,
> San Bernardino."

In this swift moving world we live in, it is true that most of us prefer to get where we are going in the fast lane, but isn't it important to have an alternate route—to escape from the road repairs—a scenic route for a leisurely drive now and then? Nobody ever wrote a song about an interstate highway!

> "Won't you get hip to this timely tip?
> When you make that California trip,
> Get your kicks on Route 66."

If it is not economically possible to restore Route 66 as an alternate route, it should be designated as an historical site. Let's get it into the history books along with other trails that have been blazed across this wonderful country we live in; The Oregon Trail—The Santa Fe trail—The Union Central/Pacific Railroad—The Kelly/Mcready first non-stop flight from New York to San Diego. Let's post signs along the new expressways reminding us that Route 66 was once here. Let us not forget our nation's most famous highway.

No Eric Zorn, not buzzard meat yet—we're not ready to play "Taps" for Route 66.

My Favorite Potato

Anyone who has ever observed a Couch Potato will agree that he/she is a truly dedicated person: the television set is appropriately placed at just the right angle for viewing ... the chair or couch, to be occupied for long periods of time, has been carefully selected for the utmost comfort ...and the tools of the trade carefully arranged on a table beside the chair or couch where he/she has squatter's rights.

I have such a person living in my house. His choice of domain is a large over-stuffed chair, which not only reclines, but swivels as well... could call him a 'Chair Potato.' On the table next to his chair he has arranged the necessary items to perform his duties: four remote controls (two for the TV, one for the VCR, and one for the stereo) ·.· two pairs of reading glasses ... a magnifying glass for small print assorted books (TV guides, pocket novels, crossword puzzles, and a dictionary) a lamp and an alarm clock. We are probably the only family in Michigan with an alarm clock in the living room. Oh well, I didn't plan to enter my home in Better Homes and Gardens anyway. Next to his chair is a rack containing his most precious possessions, his newspapers.

About eleven A.M., after retrieving the morning newspaper from between the doors where the carrier has crunched it, and pouring a cup of coffee (by then I am on my third cup) his day begins and he is ready to perform. He always reads the paper from back to front, contrary to what most people do, and out loud. Therefore, I am obliged (whether I want to or not) to listen to the current news. Of course, this way I don't have to read the newspaper for myself. When he is finished reading said paper, it is neatly folded exactly right, and filed in order of dates in the rack next to his chair.

Now at this point, he is ready to move on to other necessary things such as his morning shower and breakfast. It is then that I take advantage of his absence by removing the remains of last night's snacks covering his table and surrounding his chair. His day continues following the same pattern as above, leaving his chair now and then for unavoidable things like eating, sleeping and an occasional odd job. If someone were to be caught sitting in his chair upon his return, a long hard stare will promptly remove the occupant to another location.

I, too, have such a stare which I use as a last resort. I save it for the times when his table needs to be dusted and polished. Of course, I try other methods first: subtle hints... draping a dust cloth across the arm of his chair ... and placing the container of furniture polish on his table. If this doesn't work I use my stare. I have practiced this in the mirror to acquire just the right look, with my eyes moving back and forth from the table to his face, making sure I make eye contact. This usually has the necessary effect.

Now let me tell you about his other talents. I have observed him on many occasions, watching TV on one channel ··· taping a show on another ··· listening to the ballgame on the radio from a wire plugged into his ear ··· and reading or working a crossword puzzle during the commercials. Now I ask you, is this a dedicated Chair Potato or what?

Last night he said, "Honey, I think we should get us a portable telephone, so I won't have to get up to answer the blasted thing." I smiled sweetly at him and said, "Why not!"

Paths

It all began about twelve years ago, the summer of '78, while vacationing at our summer home on Murphy Lake. My husband was recuperating from a long illness that had caused him to take an early retirement. Our son, Pat, and our grandson, Jamie was with us. Our other children were mostly grown and had remained at home.

It had been a particularly lovely day, and had become an enchanting evening. We sat on the dock, the boys and I, in awe of the glorious sky. The starts were so brilliant it seemed we could reach up and touch them. The reflections on the water made us feel a part of the whole scene.

We sat there well into the night, unaware of time, talking about - the Big Dipper - the Little Dipper - pointing to the North Star - and Pat sharing his scientific knowledge acquired while working in the high school planetarium. Jamie had stars in his eyes, questioning as any eight year old boy would do.

I didn't sleep well that night; I had formed a picture in my mind of a small boy looking up at the stars, wonderingly. By early morning I found myself on the dock again, this time with pencil and paper in hand. Hence came the birth of my literary endeavors; my first story, written for children, "The Star Keeper."

IT is strange how one event will lead to another, taking you down a path you had never expected to explore.

I continued to write my stories (I have, at this time, completed twenty eight). However, I decided I would need illustrations to enhance them. Bing a person who could not draw a straight line, it seemed like an impossible dream. I tried to use the talents of other, but they could not quite express my ideas in their drawings.

I enrolled in a drawing class at Wayne County Community College. It opened a whole realm of possibilities. I discovered abilities I didn't know I had. Then one class led to another, another and another.

When I became a member of Poets and Play writers, a writers workshop, I was able to improve my writing. We do public readings; poetry plays and I have read my stories to children in the schools. I have been favorable received. Meanwhile, I had been working at two part-time jobs to supplement our income; one as a lunch-aid at our local elementary school, the other as a dog-groomer, Working with children and animals inspired ideas for my stories.

Four years ago another option presented itself. A friend of a friend, a writer/producer for a children's television show, "Daedal Doors" for channel 7, asked to read my stories. She thought she might be able to use me as a guest on one of her shows. I gave her copies of several to read. I didn't hear from her for several months. When I called to inquire she said, "Hand in there, you'll be hearing from me." She felt my material was good. Then a year went by. I was becoming annoyed; if she didn't want to use my stories, I certainly did want them returned. When next I spoke with her, she offered me a job as writer/producer for "Daedal Doors." I, of course, accepted. I have been able to use any talents I have developed as a writer and artist in the production of my shows. My stories have been featured on many of them.

Well here I am - late in life - in college working toward a degree in fine-arts. I have completed the illustrations of four of my books, and working on others. I don't know if they will ever be published, but I am optimistic.

Now I am contemplating an exploration down another path; Journalism. all because of one starry, starry night.

Racing with Time

Our race with time begins from the moment of birth and continues until, with our last breath, we cross the finish line.

Time however, is unimportant until we are faced with a need to recognize it; with the toll of the school-bell we are first confronted with schedules. WE must get up I the morning a the necessary time, so we can arrive at school al the designated time. Once there, it is a full day of following the school routine. Then after school there is homework-time, dinner-time, and of course bed-time, with play-time squeezed in between. This continues on into adulthood where we become clock-watchers, and are faced with deadlines each day.

So it was with me. When we married, my husband and I were both employed so there were clocks to watch. As one by one the children arrived, the work load increased. I no longer held an outside job, but work I did; by the time we had become a family of eight there just did not seem to be enough hours in my day.

Ironing is a good example of racing with time at this phase of my life. Needless to say (before polyester and perma-press) the laundry proved to be a never ending job, and the ironing a "thorn in my side."

No matter how many hours I stood at the ironing board, I never seemed to catch up. I found myself pressing last minute items of clothing late at night or early in the morning for someone to wear. Of course the older children helped at times, but the bulk of the burden was mine.

Then one dreary day as I found myself chained to the ironing board once more I thought, "There must be a better way." At that point I formulated a plan putting phase one into action; I timed myself on each item that I pressed. Moving on through shirts, pants, blouses, dresses etc., I charted my time carefully. Phase two consisted of trying to beat my time. It became a challenge and I was able to cut my time almost in half. Phase three involved sorting the clothes by priorities, into groups of items totaling the amount I could iron in on hour. Each day I dampened and ironed the designated amount. I worked for me. I found I had more time for myself, my family and other projects. I went to bed at night with a feeling o accomplishment. I realized it is easier to climb sever al small hills than to climb one mountain.

Now I know, with the discovery of polyester and perma-press, ironing is no longer an issue, but life is filled with numerous unsurmountable tasks to which this same principal can often be applied; if we climb the small hiss—one hill at a time—one day at a time—we will eventually reach the top of the mountain.

As I continue my race with time, the finish line not yet in sight, I will conclude this train of thought with my poem titled (you guessed it) Time.

Summer's End

As summer dwindles away, I sit here watching the sun slowly descending behind the horizon. I listen to a robin singing his last song of the day... probably contemplating the long inevitable flight. The words, 'free as a bird' come to mind. He doesn't have to make a reservation, pack a bag or service his car. He doesn't have to make the decision of where to go this winter to get away from the cold. He instinctively knows. He doesn't have to wonder what kind of clothing to take for whatever kind of weather he might encounter. He certainly doesn't have to choose a motel for an overnight stopover. No credit cards. Just lift his wings and 'fly with the birds.'

But, for us humans the end of summer also means inevitable change. We have mixed emotions about summer's end. I personally am not sad for I love the autumn season with all its splendor. To me there is nothing like the smell of the fresh invigorating air of fall, the beauty of the leaves changing colors, and the sound as we crunch them underfoot. My heart soars as I watch the geese following their leader in perfect formation. That is true freedom.

But for now, I will not think beyond this glorious summer's eve. I will not think about the winter's cold and snow. I am free to drink in and savor nature's winding

211

down of summer. I look forward to the changing seasons. And even when old man winter is challenging us with his with his fiercest chill, I know, 'when winter comes, spring will not be far behind!'

(c) 1996

Prankster

Due to all the detours, they had been driving for hours without having seen a single abode, not even a barn. The gas was running low, and it certainly was no place to get stranded in the storm that was deluging them. They needed to find a place to spend the night, so when they came across the abandoned house nestled in a grove of trees; Tom turned onto the long winding trail and parked. "Come on, honey, grab your overnight bag and a blanket ... maybe we can get inside out of the rain."

"But, it looks so ... so spooky, Tom who knows what we'll find in there." When her husband of one day stepped out of the car, Carol had no choice to follow, almost tripping over the For Sale sign that lay flat on the ground.

The door was locked but that didn't deter Tom, he pulled a loose board from the front window and after clearing away the shards of shattered glass, carefully crawled through window. When Carol finally heard the creaky front door open, she was relieved to see her new husband standing in the doorway.

After exploring, they discovered the electricity was shut off. The rooms were sparsely large well-worn sofa and get some sleep.

The sound of the laughter woke them with a start. Where was it coming from? They were sure there was so one in the house. But, before Torn could investigate, the sofa, with them still sitting on it, rose up in the air, almost touching the ceiling. It circled the room, spinning around

213

like a top! Carol was terrified. Tom held her close. Was it a POLTERGEIST? The laughter continued, louder and louder!

At long last the sofa dropped to the floor with a thud. The laughter stopped. "Let's get out of here, Tom!" He agreed picking up their bags and the blanket. They hurried to the door, but when they tried to open it, the laughter began again and the door wouldn't open! No matter how hard he tried, it wouldn't budge. When he approached the broken window the boards were back in place and the laughter became louder ... almost deafening. They hurried to the back door, it wouldn't open either! The laughter seemed to surround them. Carol screamed, "Stop, let us out! It's not funny." The laughter continued. "Tom, what are we going to do?"

"Maybe," Tom suggested, "if we ignore it, it will go away." When they returned to the living room, the front door stood open. Tom made a dash for it, but before he could reach it, the door slammed shut, and he couldn't get it open again! "Damn," he swore. "What do you want from us?" More laughter.

Carol slumped down on the sofa once more. "I don't think it means to harm us, honey." He held her close. Everything was quiet for a while so decided to rest. About the time they were almost asleep, it began again. Only this time it was the windows. The windows all over the house opened and slammed shut as Tom approached them one by one. The laughter began all over again. Tom was frustrated as he dashed from one window to another. Finally unable to stand it any longer, he raised his fists and shouted, "Have it your way! Don't you know this is our honeymoon!"

Suddenly silence. Then, as if having to get the last word in, it ended with a loud, ooooooooooooooooooooooh"

And they slept.

When they awoke, the sun was streaming in. As Tom crossed to the door it creaked open. "Carol," he called to his bride, "let's get out of here." He held the door open for her so it wouldn't close again, and they hurried to the car. But as the car fish-tailed down the rutted driveway, Carol turned for one last look.

"Look!" Carol shouted. Tom turned to look. The whole house shook with laughter! They turned toward each other laughing so hard tears were sliding down their faces. This would be a story to tell their grandchildren ...someday!

The Tree

Buddy stood there before us clutching what seemed to be a very young sapling. Although it could easily have been mistaken for a weed, it was indeed a tree. Our small son, brown eyes sparkling, face smudged with dirt, baseball cap askew was extremely excited about this wonderful find. The knees of his jeans were soiled and torn from kneeling in the dirt while digging up his treasure. He had found the tree in the field near the creek at the end of our street. He had been forbidden to go there alone, but not wanting to spoil this moment, we decided to postpone the lecture on this issue until later.

Roots dangled limply from the tree he held in his grubby fist. It was his contribution to our attempts at landscaping. We had moved into our new home several months before and had, at last, managed to coax our lawn into existence. We had planted two trees; a maple and a tulip tree in the front yard for shade, and shrubs across the front of the house for beautification. In the back yard stood a peach tree and another shade tree of unknown origin. We really did not need another tree.

Now, here was Buddy with his gift of love. We praised it profusely, identifying it as a poplar tree. After a lengthy discussion about where to plant it, we decided to give it a place of prominence; next to the driveway on the grassy stretch near the curb. We felt it probably wouldn't grow anyway ⋯ but grow it did!

After four long years, Bud returned home safely from the war. He married, moving on to another life. When the umbilical cord between mother and son finally severed, the link between the boy and his tree no longer existed.

It was about then that we began to see the tree for what it really was; a pesky poplar tree. Its cotton-like seeds polluting the air, and its roots causing the sidewalk and driveway to heave. We decided it had to be removed.

Yet when the teeth of the power saw bit into its trunk, I felt a tug at my heart strings. I remembered a day long ago, when a small boy, brown eyes sparkling, baseball cap askew, clutched a young tree in his grubby fist. The picture will remain with me forever.

Printed in the United States
By Bookmasters